what if someone i know is gay?

what if someone i know is gay?

ANSWERS TO QUESTIONS ABOUT WHAT IT MEANS TO BE GAY AND LESBIAN

ERIC MARCUS

SIMON PULSE

New York   London   Toronto   Sydney

SIMON PULSE

An imprint of Simon & Schuster Children's Publishing Division

1230 Avenue of the Americas, New York, NY 10020

Copyright © 2000, 2007 by Eric Marcus

An earlier edition of this work was published in 2000

by Price Stern Sloan, a division of

Penguin Putnam Books for Young Readers.

SIMON PULSE and colophon are registered trademarks

of Simon & Schuster, Inc.

Designed by Mike Rosamilia

The text of this book was set in Gotham Book.

Manufactured in the United States of America

First Simon Pulse edition August 2007

2 4 6 8 10 9 7 5 3 1

Library of Congress Control Number 00-108447

ISBN-13: 978-1-4169-4970-1

ISBN-10: 1-4169-4970-4

At long last,
a book for Rachel

CONTENTS

introduction

*W*hat *If Someone I Know Is Gay?* is an introductory book about gay people. I've tried to do my best to answer a lot of the questions you might have, from "How do you become gay?" to "Can gay people get married?" Some of the questions are very obvious, some not so obvious, and you might even find a few that you think are stupid. But the way I see it, there's no such thing as a stupid question, except the one you don't ask.

Many of the questions you'll find in this book are questions I've been asked by friends, family, and colleagues. Other questions have been asked of me in my role as an author by people who have written to me or e-mailed me after reading one of my books. And several of the questions you'll find here have come in response to an e-mail request I sent asking people to contribute their questions.

✳ Why did you write this book?

An editor at a publishing company read a book that I wrote for adults called *Is It a Choice? Answers to the Most Frequently Asked Questions About Gay & Lesbian People*, and she thought it would be great if I could write a book specifically for young adults. And I was glad to do it, because when it comes to the subject of gay and lesbian people and gay issues, there are a lot of questions that never get asked and a lot of answers that never get offered.

I think we'd all be a lot better off if everyone could ask whatever questions they had and could count on getting honest answers in return. I remember being in kindergarten and asking my teacher why a sixth grader was sent to our class to stand in the corner for an hour one morning. I thought it was a perfectly reasonable question. My teacher, whose name I can't recall (I'm sure I'm blocking it), told me to mind my own business. I think it was this embarrassing and hurtful experience that helped fuel my curiosity about life and set me on the path of asking questions for a living.

✳ Who is it for?

This book is for anyone who knows someone gay. That means it's for everyone, because everyone knows someone who is gay: a sister or brother, parent, teacher, neighbor, classmate, or friend. Or maybe you're gay yourself or think you might be.

Of course a lot of people don't realize they know someone who is gay or lesbian because many gay people hide the fact that they're gay. Why? That's a good question, and it's just one of the many that I answer in this book.

✳ Who are you? And how did you get to be an expert?

Often when I get e-mails from readers they want to know who I am. I'm used to asking other people about their lives and keeping private about my own. But it's only fair if you're reading my book for you to know who is offering the answers, especially because a lot of the answers reflect my personal opinions. (I don't speak for any organizations, political parties, companies, or religious groups. I speak for myself and no one else.)

I grew up with my brother and sister in a small neighborhood in Queens, which is a part of New York City. I went to public schools and then to Vassar College, where I majored in urban studies. I have a master's degree in journalism from Columbia University and a second master's degree from Columbia's Graduate School of Architecture, Planning and Preservation.

I wrote my first book, a guide for male couples, when I was in my late twenties. And I can tell you that I was no expert on gay people at that time, but as I discovered when the book was first published, I had to have answers to the basic questions about gay issues that reporters asked me because in those days, people didn't know a lot about gay people (and the reporters were even more nervous asking the questions than I was answering them!).

So I became an expert through my work, but since I'm also gay, I've had a lot of incentive to learn about gay people and gay life so I could better understand myself—especially since when I was growing up there was very little information available that could help a gay young person understand himself and the kind of life he could expect to lead.

Since 1988 I've written several books about gay men and women and gay relationships. I also coauthored a couple of autobiographies of gay athletes, including Greg Louganis, an Olympic diving champion. And I wrote an award-winning oral history of the gay civil rights movement called *Making Gay History*. (You can learn more about my books on my website, www.ericmarcus.com.)

My partner and I met in December 1993 and we had a commitment ceremony in June 1996. (A commitment ceremony is like a wedding, but we didn't use a rabbi or priest and we didn't get a marriage license because gay people couldn't get married anywhere in the United States in those days.) We had more than two hundred guests, and everyone in our families attended. We don't have children, but we have nieces and nephews we're close to and we've got great friends.

✳ Did you write this book by yourself?

I had the help of a lot of people in writing this book, from both experts and regular people.

✳ Who are the people you write about?

In the book you'll find stories about people from all over the country, mostly young people, both gay and straight. And there are comments from a few adults, mostly parents.

When it comes to the people I identify by name, all the adults who asked that I use their names are identified by their full names. For all the young people who spoke with me, I've used only first names and I've changed all of these names, as well as some identifying characteristics. Most of the young people I talked to wanted me to use their real first names or their full names, but I prefer that they remain anonymous. It's difficult to know what will happen once your name is in print, and given the still controversial nature of this subject, I think it's safer for the young people I write about to stay out of the public eye.

✳ What if I can't find answers to my questions? Where can I get more information?

Since this is only an introductory book, you may not find the answers to *all* of your questions. So in the last chapter you'll find lots of resources, including books, organizations, and websites. If after checking out these resources you still can't get the information you need or there's a question that still needs answering, write to me and I'll do my best to help you.

✳ How can I contact you?

You can write to me through my website, www.ericmarcus.com. Or e-mail me directly at eric@ericmarcus.com.

chapter 1
the basic stuff

I like to think that the best place to start when you're new to any subject (and even if you're not entirely new) is at the beginning. Homosexuality is a complicated and all too often controversial subject that's difficult to discuss if you don't understand the basic concepts and issues. So I've devoted this first chapter, which is the longest in the book, to all the essential questions (and answers) you need to know before reading the chapters that follow. You may be tempted to skip right to the chapter about sex, but I urge you to start here.

Before you get to the first question, I have a quick warning about the Internet that you've no doubt heard before from your parents, but bears repeating because throughout this chapter and the ones that follow, I recommend various websites. So here's the warning: It is extremely important to be cautious when you use the Internet, especially if you decide to join a discussion group or use the Internet to meet other young people. Because it's so easy to create a false online profile, it can be hard to tell who is being truthful and who is not. So there's the possibility that someone may try to take advantage of you, may make you uncomfortable online, or might try to arrange to meet you when they should not.

Always remember that when meeting people online, you should use the same caution you would when meeting any stranger: Never give out your telephone number or home address and never agree to meet anyone in person unless you are accompanied by a parent or another responsible adult, and then only meet in a public place.

The Internet is an amazing resource, but you have to be careful and use common sense when you go online. And, if possible, please seek guidance from your parents or a responsible adult.

✳ What does "gay" mean?

Someone who is attracted to people of the same sex is "gay" or "homosexual" (these words can refer to both men and women, although a lot of women prefer to be called "lesbian"). Someone who is attracted to people of the opposite sex is called "heterosexual" or "straight." And someone who is attracted to people of both the same sex and the opposite sex is called "bisexual." "Gay," "straight," and "bisexual" are all terms that describe a person's "sexual orientation." And sexual orientation simply refers to the sex (or gender) of the people you're attracted to. In other words, if your sexual orientation is gay, then you are attracted to someone of the same sex.

✳ How do you become gay?

Simple answer: You can't *become* gay, just like you can't *become* straight. This is how it works: All of us have feelings of sexual attraction. Most of us have these feelings for people of the opposite sex—boys for girls, girls for boys. Some of us have these feelings for people of the same sex—boys for boys, girls for girls. And some people have feelings of sexual attraction for both the same sex and the opposite sex.

For example, when Mae was ten years old, she already knew she was different from most of her classmates. "All the girls in elementary school were boy crazy. I knew that I wasn't, but I pretended to be like everyone else."

No one knows exactly how we come by our feelings of sexual attraction in the first place, but whether we're born with them or develop them in the early years of life, they are a gift that can make us feel very good as well as very confused.

As we enter our teen years, these feelings of attraction grow stronger and we often find ourselves both emotionally and physically—or sexually—attracted to another person. That was Mae's experience. By the time she was thirteen, her feelings of sexual attraction were clear. "When I was thirteen I admitted it to myself. My friends were always talking about being attracted to cute guys. And I was always just attracted to girls. It was a feeling inside. I tried to be attracted to guys, but it wasn't working."

✳ **What exactly are "feelings of sexual attraction"?**
As we grow into adolescence and our bodies change, we begin to have strong feelings of attraction that are different from and more intense than the good feelings we might have for a relative or friend. It is these strong feelings of sexual attraction that make us want to have a sexual relationship. For some people these feelings begin before puberty, and for others they don't come until after. These special feelings of excitement and desire are difficult to describe, but you'll know them when you experience them.

Looking back, I can tell you exactly when I had strong feelings of sexual attraction for the first time. I didn't know what to call it then, because I'd never experienced anything like it before, but I knew that I was feeling something very powerful that made me feel really good in a way that's difficult to describe.

I was twelve and a half and I was in Puerto Rico with my family on vacation (it was our first trip where we had to take an airplane). I was in the swimming pool at the Caribe Hilton, hanging out in the shallow end. I wasn't much of a swimmer and couldn't float very well. This older kid, who was probably sixteen or seventeen and a really good swimmer, must have noticed that I was trying to float on my back but kept sinking and getting water up my nose. So he swam over and offered to teach me how to float. Turns out that Andrew was a lifeguard back home and he was really good-looking, but I don't remember thinking, *Oh, he's cute.*

What I *do* remember is that Andrew got me to float on my back. Before I could sink like I always did, he put one hand under the base of my back and his other hand between my shoulder blades and applied just enough pressure to keep me from going under. And he told me to relax as he walked me around the pool to get me comfortable with being on my back in the water.

It wasn't like lightning struck or anything, but it felt as if there was energy that started in Andrew's hands and traveled through my entire body. It was a wonderful, tingly feeling, which made my heart race and made me feel calm all at the same time. It felt *so* good that I wished I could float in the pool all day with Andrew's hands supporting me.

I look back now and I can tell you that I was definitely having feelings of sexual attraction for the first time in my life. And those feelings were so powerful that I can recall the experience and those feelings like it was yesterday.

✳ What is sex?

You've probably noticed that the word "sex" has more than one meaning. It can refer to a person's gender—in other words, whether a person is male or female. It can also refer to something two people do together when they're attracted to each other. (You can read more about that in Chapter 4, "Sex.")

✳ Is being gay a choice?

I'm asked this question more often than just about any other, and the answer is *no*. People don't choose their feelings of sexual attraction. That's true for *everyone*. I didn't choose to feel the way I did when Andrew touched me, and if you've ever been attracted to someone, whether they're of the same sex or the opposite sex, you know that you didn't decide to feel tingly whenever you were near them. Like your eye color, skin color, or height, you don't get to choose your feelings of sexual attraction. They have been chosen for you. However, what you decide to *do* about these feelings is a matter of choice.

✳ Can you change your feelings?

No. When it comes to feelings of sexual attraction, no amount of hoping, praying, counseling, or wishful thinking will make them go away. Unlike most gifts, when it comes to your feelings of sexual attraction, there are no exchanges and no returns. You can try to ignore your feelings, you can pretend you're not having them, but no matter what anyone says, you can't change or eliminate your feelings of sexual attraction, just as you can't change the true color of your eyes. That goes for gay people just as it does for straight people.

I remember being thirteen and hoping that my feelings for people of the same sex would change. At the time, I had a crush on my camp counselor, Ted. I didn't just like Ted—I really, really liked Ted. It's not that I wanted to have sex with him—I wasn't even certain how people had sex. But I wanted to be around Ted, I thought about him all the time, and it made me feel very good the few times he put his arm around my shoulder.

I was pretty sure that the other boys in my cabin didn't feel the way I did. For one thing, they talked a lot about Ted's girlfriend, Rebecca, a counselor in the teen division, who they thought looked amazing in a bathing suit. I could tell Rebecca was attractive, but I didn't understand what all the excitement was about. I especially didn't understand why my cabin-mates were all so interested in going on late-night raids of the girls' cabins.

At first I didn't worry too much about my crush on Ted and other guys, because I'd heard that some boys have these feelings and outgrow them. (How our feelings of sexual attraction develop is more complicated than that, as you'll find out in the answer to the next question, but in general gay kids can't "outgrow" whom they are sexually attracted to any more than straight kids can.) But I quickly learned from the other kids at camp that my attraction to guys was something really nasty, so I was hoping I'd outgrow those feelings fast. I figured that I would stop having crushes on male counselors and would start having crushes on girl counselors, and that one day I even might want to get up in the middle of the night and crawl through the woods to the other side of camp and sneak into one of the girls' cabins. But as much as I hoped that my feelings would change, they didn't.

✳ What about people who say they used to be gay, but now they're not? Did they really change?

There are people who say that they used to be gay or lesbian and that they've changed or been "cured" through prayer, through counseling, or by attending a program designed to help gay people become "ex-gays." It is true that people *can* change their behavior. But they can't change their true feelings of sexual attraction. Those feelings, no matter how hard you might try to bury them, ignore them, or convince yourself you don't have them, stay with you for as long as you live.

For example, a gay man can end his relationship with

another man and start having a relationship with a woman. But that doesn't mean he's suddenly developed feelings of sexual attraction for women. In all likelihood he still has the same attraction to men that he always had. He may be trying to ignore those feelings, but they're still there.

I remember getting a letter many years ago from a former boyfriend who went through an "ex-gay" program. He wrote to me just after my first book, *The Male Couple's Guide*, was published. He told me that I could choose to change too, just like he had. But I had long since decided to be true to myself and had no interest in trying to be something I wasn't. I knew that society would be more accepting of me if I pretended to be straight, but I thought it would be better to use my energy to fight prejudice than to fight against my true feelings. After all, there is nothing wrong with my feelings, so why try to pretend I don't have them?

I hope I've been clear on this point: Whether you're straight or gay, you can't change your feelings of sexual attraction. When you're young, it's perfectly natural to have a range of feelings, including feelings of same-sex attraction. These feelings may evolve, but by your late teens, you're usually sure of those feelings and there's nothing you can do to change them. However, our sexual natures are complex, so just because *you* can't change your feelings of sexual attraction doesn't mean they won't go and change on their own as you go through life. Please keep in mind that this is *not* a typical experience, and from my experiences talking to people over the years, it's something you're far more likely to hear from a girl than a guy.

For example, Molly told everyone she was a lesbian when she was sixteen years old. She had a girlfriend all through college, but after they broke up (when Molly was twenty-three), she found herself becoming interested in guys. "I still think women are beautiful," she says, "but I haven't met a woman who moves me like men have moved me in the last seven years or so. I can't explain it." I can't explain it either, but Molly says that she truly feels sexually attracted to men, which she didn't when she was younger.

✳ How can I tell if I'm gay, lesbian, or bisexual? Do you just wake up one day and discover that you're gay?

No, you don't just wake up one day and discover that you're gay—just as you don't wake up one day and discover that you're straight. But finding a label for yourself isn't nearly as important as trying to sort out your feelings, and that can take time. For some people, their feelings of sexual attraction are clear from an early age, as young as five or six. But for most, it's something they become aware of during adolescence or later, and that's the same whether you're attracted to someone of the same sex, the opposite sex, or both.

Jake, who is now seventeen and finishing his last year of high school, knew very early. "I always knew I was attracted to other guys, as far back as kindergarten. I just was. I was always curious about doing sexual stuff with other boys." Michelle also knew early, but it wasn't that she wanted to have sex with other girls. "That came later," she said. "From the time I was six I knew I was going to marry a girl. I told my parents and they said, 'That's nice, honey.' They weren't taking me seriously. I was only six. So I told them over and over again. They tried telling me I was going to marry a boy when I grew up, but I just shook my head no 'cause I knew they were wrong."

Kevin, a high school junior from southern California, wasn't really sure of his sexual feelings until he was in his early teens, although by the time he was ten he knew he was different from most other boys. "But I didn't have a word for it," he told me. "I just knew. When the girls and boys started to interact, I felt totally out of place. It didn't make sense to me."

Jennifer, a nineteen-year-old college sophomore, found herself attracted to other girls at her Catholic high school. "I looked at girls and saw them as really attractive," she said, "and I wanted to be with them in more ways than just friends. I was sexually attracted to them." But Jennifer was confused by her feelings. She explained: "You're taught in society to go after the opposite sex, to date the opposite sex. I thought I was going to be a part of that. It finally took meeting another girl who was gay, and talking to her about what it was like to be gay, for me to realize I wasn't going to do what society told me. That was just a few months ago. And now I know for sure I don't want to pretend to be someone else."

For many people the pressure "to go after the opposite sex" keeps them from recognizing or understanding their true feelings. They want to be like everyone else, which is a natural impulse. They don't want to feel left out and alone and they don't want to have romantic and/or sexual feelings that some people think are bad. Given these circumstances, many kids and teenagers need time and the experiences of growing up to sort out and accept what they really feel.

I'd like to say that I was one of those people who did a good job of sorting things out and didn't go through a period of trying to be straight and wanting to fit in. But that's not true. I didn't want to be gay and I did want to fit in, so along the way I badly hurt the feelings of a girl I dated during my first semester of college. I wasn't honest with her about what was going on in my head, so she had no way of knowing that the primary problem in our relationship was that I was gay *and* dishonest about it. In the years since, we've become very good friends, but I think it's still something of a sore spot for her that I didn't trust her enough to tell her that I was seriously conflicted about my sexual orientation.

✳ Are people who are bisexual attracted to men and women in the same way?

No. For most people who consider themselves bisexual, their feelings of sexual attraction are usually stronger for one sex than the other. For example, David is a nineteen-year-old college student who considers himself bisexual, but he's mostly attracted to men. "Right now I have a boyfriend, but I also really like women. I'm more sexually attracted to men, but there are certain women I find really attractive and I'm more comfortable with them emotionally. I don't know, but that's how I feel."

Another example is Helen, who is also a college student who finds men more sexually attractive than women, but in the past she's been attracted to women, too, and had a girlfriend for a short time. "I think I'll probably wind up with a guy, but you never know. If I fall in love with a woman first, that could be it. But I'm not in any rush to settle down with anyone for a long time."

✳ I thought bisexuals were just gay people who were confused or afraid to admit they're gay. Is that true?

Some people think that men and women who call them-selves bisexual are really gay but are just afraid to say it. While it's true that some gay men and women adopt the "bisexual" label as they're sorting out and learning to accept their true feelings—I was one of those people—there are in fact some people who have feelings of sexual attraction for both men and women. These people are not confused, afraid, or pretending. They're simply bisexual.

✳ Do you have to have sex to know if you're gay or not?

No, most people, gay or straight, have a pretty good idea of what their feelings of sexual attraction are long before they have a sexual experience with anyone. You can know just from how you feel inside. But sometimes it takes a sexual and/or emotional experience for someone to understand and recognize what their true feelings are. For example, over the years I've interviewed many women who said they knew they felt different but didn't realize what that difference was until they fell in love with another woman for the first time and/or had a sexual experience with a woman.

The men I've talked to, in general, had a clearer idea at an earlier age of what their feelings of attraction were, so a sexual experience only confirmed for them what they already knew to be true. For example, I remember kissing girls at summer camp and thinking it was nice, but nothing all that special, at least not as special as the other boys seemed to think it was. At that age I didn't think of myself as gay, although I knew I had crushes on some of my male counselors.

I still didn't want to think of myself as gay when I was seventeen and had a crush on Bob, a gay college student who lived down the street. Given how bad I thought it was to be gay, I was trying hard to ignore my feelings. But those feelings were very strong, and when I finally kissed Bob, that was it. It felt like the most natural thing in the world for me, and it was amazing. For the first time I really understood why the boys at camp would want to get up in the middle of the night and crawl through the woods in the hope of getting to kiss a girl. It's just that I felt that way about a guy, and after that first experience, there was no doubt in my mind that I was gay—but it was still a few years before I completely accepted that these were my true feelings and that they weren't going to change, whether I liked it or not.

✳ Why can't you just pretend that you're not gay?

Plenty of people who are gay pretend that they're straight, at least for a time. But it's not easy. In fact, it's just as difficult for someone who is gay to pretend to be straight as it would be for someone who is straight to pretend to be gay.

For example, just imagine for a few minutes that you live in a world where most people are gay. That's a fun thing to imagine for someone who is gay, but what if you're a straight guy and you don't want anyone to know that you're different from most people? Well, you can never talk about the girls you're attracted to. You have to bring a male date to the junior prom. And when you get older, you'll be expected to marry a guy and have sex with him. How easy would it be for you to pretend?

In years past, when gay and lesbian people faced far more prejudice and weren't nearly as accepted as they are now, most pretended they were straight for their entire lives. Often that included getting married to someone of the opposite sex and having children. But, as many people have discovered, pretending to be someone you're not can be incredibly difficult and can make you and the people around you very unhappy.

✳ If you have been sexually abused, can that make you gay?

No. Some people think that you can become gay if you have been sexually abused or if you have a bad sexual experience with someone of the opposite sex. They are wrong. Sexual abuse or a bad sexual experience can color how you feel about people who are the same gender as the abuser or the person with whom you had the bad experience. Being abused or having a bad experience can make you angry, confused, or saddened by what's happened to you, but your feelings of sexual attraction—your sexual orientation—cannot be changed as a result of sexual abuse or a bad sexual experience. Unfortunately, many young people experience sexual abuse, and most of them turn out to be straight, because most people are straight.

✳ If I think I'm gay, lesbian, or bisexual, what should I do?

It's a good idea to learn as much as you can about what it means to be gay and to find someone you can talk to who is knowledgeable and trustworthy so you won't feel so alone, which is a problem for a lot of young gay people who write to me.

The first thing you should do is read the rest of this book and see if you can find some of the books I've listed in Chapter 9, "Resources." You should also have a look at some of the websites I recommend, which provide all kinds of information, including where you may be able to find organizations for young people in your community. Some of the websites also offer opportunities to meet other young people who are gay, lesbian, and bisexual, but I do not recommend this unless you talk to your parents or another responsible adult first or are old enough to do this on your own. (Always remember that when meeting people online, you should use the same caution you would when meeting any stranger. See the beginning of this chapter and Chapter 9, "Resources," for a more complete warning.)

I know that many young people who think they're gay,

lesbian, or bisexual are afraid they're all alone. But you're not alone. The challenge is finding someone you can talk to whom you can trust and who will understand what you're feeling. That person may be a teacher, school counselor, friend, or relative. If you're lucky, there may be a GSA (Gay-Straight Alliance) at your high school or a gay youth support group in your community or a chapter of PFLAG (Parents, Families and Friends of Lesbians and Gays) nearby. At all of these organizations, you'll find people you can talk to who understand what you're going through.

One thing to consider if you're afraid to let anyone know who you are is that you can also seek help without sharing your name or contact information. For example, you can e-mail or call PFLAG and explain that you need to talk to a parent for advice but have to remain anonymous because you can't risk anyone finding out that you're gay. I've received plenty of e-mails over the years from people who were in exactly that situation, and I've had no problem offering advice without knowing the real name of the person who contacted me.

✳ Is it true that being gay is like a disease?

No. Homosexuality is not a disease or sickness. But as shocking as it may seem today, years ago people who had feelings of same-sex attraction were considered mentally ill by most mental health professionals and the general public. Then, in the early 1970s, the American Psychological

Association and the American Psychiatric Association each recognized that they'd made a mistake (a huge mistake!) and removed homosexuality from the list of mental illnesses.

Still, there are a small number of psychiatrists and psychologists who mistakenly believe that gay and lesbian people are by nature mentally ill and that they can be "cured." These people are considered by their peers to be far outside the mainstream of their professions, and their work to "cure" homosexuality is not supported by our current understandings of human sexuality. These misguided psychiatrists and psychologists hold out false hope to those gay and lesbian people who are unhappy with being gay and are searching for a "cure." Homosexuality is not an illness, so there is nothing to be cured.

✳ I've heard that being gay is "bad" or "nasty." Is that true?

No, this is not true. Homosexuality is not bad or nasty. But many people have been taught to believe this by their families, friends, and religious leaders. These beliefs are based on ancient myths and misunderstandings about the nature of homosexuality and misunderstandings about the ways in which gay and lesbian people lead their lives.

Much to my surprise, several years ago my own nephew was shocked to learn that my partner and I were gay.

He had always known us as a couple, but no one had ever said that we were "gay." And when his cousin, Rachel, asked him if he knew that his uncles were gay, he asked his dad (my brother), who told him that Rachel was telling the truth. Ryan was very confused, because, as he said to his dad, "I thought 'gay' was something nasty." The full story of what happened with my nephew is on my website in an article called "Don't Be So Gay."

✳ Is homosexuality abnormal?

To answer that question, we have to figure out what the word "abnormal" means. Some people feel something is abnormal if it's unusual. Given how many gay and lesbian people there are, we know that it's not unusual. Here's another example: Even though most people are right-handed, we don't consider left-handed people abnormal. They're simply different from the majority. Years ago, left-handed people (like my dad) were thought to be abnormal or defective, just as many people today still believe that gay men and women are abnormal. Like left-handedness, being gay is simply different from the majority and is absolutely normal.

You might think something is abnormal if it's unnatural. Being gay or lesbian is natural by definition, because it occurs in nature—and not just among humans. Scientists have studied all kinds of animals that engage in homosexual behavior, from mountain rams and seagulls to gorillas. Also, gay and lesbian people who are comfortable with their sexuality will tell you that their experience of having a sexual relationship with someone of the same sex feels perfectly natural to them, just as natural as it is for straight people to have a sexual relationship with someone of the opposite sex.

✳ My minister says that homosexuality is immoral and sinful. What do you think?

I don't believe that homosexuality is immoral or sinful, and many religious leaders agree. But morality and religious beliefs are a matter of personal choice, something that each of us must decide on his or her own. (See Chapter 5, "God and Religion," for more on this topic.)

✳ Do gay boys look at other boys in the locker room? Do lesbians look at other girls in the locker room?

Yes, and straight boys look at other boys, and straight girls look at other girls. People are curious by nature, whether they're straight or gay, especially during puberty, when their bodies are changing. So when it comes to the locker room, most boys look at other boys and most girls look at other girls. This is true whether you're in middle school, college, or at a neighborhood gym.

Is it possible that the gay kid in the locker room is looking at you because he or she is gay and finds you attractive? That's always a possibility (and in that case, you can think of the attention as a compliment), but more likely than not, he or she is just curious about the way you look in the same way that all humans are curious.

✳ Are there a lot of gay and lesbian people?

Yes, there are. But since a lot of gay and lesbian people remain hidden—they don't talk about it, or they pretend that they're straight—no one knows exactly how many gay men and women there are. From all I've read over the years, I believe that about 3 percent of men are gay and about 1.5 percent of women are lesbian (no one knows why there are about half the number of lesbians as there are gay men). So if you accept my guesstimate, that means there are 9 million gay men and 4.5 million lesbians in the United States. To put that in perspective, 2 percent of the U.S. population is Jewish, which is a little more than 6 million people.

Whatever the exact number, there are tens of millions of gay people around the world, and the odds are that there are gay men and women in every extended family.

✳ Where do they live?

Gay and lesbian people live in all parts of the country and in every community. But for a long time, many gay people have chosen to live in big cities, and they've done so for several reasons. Some gay people left their small towns and cities to get away from families and communities where they feared and/or experienced prejudice. Others chose to live in big cities because they wanted to be in places where there were many more chances to meet other gay people like themselves. And because of the large numbers of gay men and women living in the big cities, there are also many different kinds of gay and lesbian organizations for people to join, from sports clubs and political organizations to gay and lesbian churches and synagogues.

In recent years, as prejudice has decreased and gay men and lesbians have felt more comfortable being themselves, fewer have felt the need to leave their home communities and cities to move to larger cities simply because of their sexual orientation.

✳ What kind of future can you have if you're lesbian or gay?

Jennifer, who grew up in Denver and now attends college in northern Colorado, told me: "I see myself living a happy life, with a long-term relationship. I see living the same life as my sister, only she'll be married to a guy and I'll be married to a girl."

Jennifer, like most young gay and lesbian people, can look forward to a life much the same as any young person, despite remaining prejudice. But because of that prejudice, many parents worry that their gay and lesbian children may face more challenges than their straight brothers and sisters.

When my mother first found out I was gay, she told me that she was sad that I'd never have a happy relationship. I pointed out that from what I could tell, being straight didn't seem to be any guarantee of having a happy relationship: She and my father separated when I was ten. But my mother's concern was genuine. It was 1977 when my mother learned I was gay, and she didn't know any gay or lesbian couples (and neither did I, for that matter). She was concerned that because of discrimination against gay people, I'd have fewer career opportunities. She was also afraid that people would look down on me. My mom asked if I had any idea how much more difficult my life would be, and I didn't really have an answer for her, because I didn't know. But I did know that no matter how hard it might be, hiding the fact I was gay or pretending to be straight would be harder.

Today we know that gay people have loving, long-lasting relationships; more and more gay and lesbian people are choosing to have children of their own (something that often makes the potential grandparents very happy); openly gay people hold jobs in just about any profession you can imagine (with the major exception of the U.S. military, which still actively discriminates against openly gay men and lesbians); and while many straight people look down on gay people, with each passing year, more and more are discovering that gay men and lesbians are just like everyone else, especially in their hopes and dreams for the future.

✳ How can you tell if someone is gay or lesbian? Do people look gay or lesbian or act a certain way?

Most young people think they can tell if someone is gay, but take my word for it: Most of the time, you can't.

When I was growing up, I thought that all gay men were feminine and that all lesbians were masculine, so I figured that you could always tell. It turns out that the truth is more complicated than that. While some gay men are feminine and some lesbians are masculine, most are no different in manner and appearance from the average straight man or woman, so it's generally difficult to look at someone and be able to tell whether or not he or she is gay.

Something to think about: Not all feminine men are gay and not all masculine women are lesbians. At the same time, not all masculine men and not all feminine women are straight. As I said, the truth is complicated.

✳ If you're a gay boy, do you eventually act and talk like a girl? If you're a lesbian, do you become masculine and get very athletic?

No. In general, gay men who are feminine and lesbians who are masculine were born that way. They are not trying to be feminine or masculine. They are just being themselves.

✳ Do gay men want to be women? Do lesbians want to be men?

No. Gay men are happy being male, and lesbians are happy being female. People who don't feel comfortable with their gender—in other words, people who were born male who feel like they're really girls, or people who were born female who feel like they're really boys—are called "transgender." You can find more information about transgender people by checking out some of the resources I recommend in Chapter 9, "Resources."

✳ Are transgender people gay?

Just like anyone else, transgender people can be straight, gay, or bisexual. How people experience being male or female has nothing to do with their feelings of sexual attraction for others.

✳ What does it mean when a gay person "comes out"?

"Coming out" or "coming out of the closet" means to tell the truth about your sexual orientation—to yourself, to friends, to family, or to anyone who doesn't know that you're gay or lesbian. In other words, before I came out to my friends, I was hiding the truth from them (sort of like hiding my true self in a closet). When I felt comfortable about being gay and trusted that my friends would still love me if they knew the truth, I came out to them.

✳ How old are gay people when they come out?

Some people come out when they're ten years old. Others never come out. But these days, many—if not most—gay people come out to themselves and their friends and family when they're in high school or college.

✳ What does "outing" mean?

Let's say you're gay and you don't want anyone to know about it, except maybe your closest friends and family. Then, someone who knows that you're gay decides to tell everyone at school the truth about your sexual orientation. That's "outing" someone. It means revealing the truth about a gay person's sexual orientation against their wishes or without their permission. With rare exceptions for hypocritical politicians and religious leaders, I've always believed that it's up to the individual person to decide to come out or stay in the closet, whether it's a teenager from Nebraska or a Hollywood celebrity. Forcing someone out of the closet who isn't ready to come out is, in general, a cruel thing to do and it's wrong.

✳ Why do some straight people think that gay people should stay in the closet?

Some people think that being gay is so wrong and sinful that gay men and women should be embarrassed to reveal the truth. Some think that an openly gay relative will reflect badly on family members if other people know about it. Others think that if gay people are public about their sexual orientation, they'll somehow be a bad influence on children. Still others are concerned that if someone they care about is openly gay, he or she may be subject to prejudice and mistreatment. And some people haven't really thought about why, but they just wish gay people would go back to being invisible the way they were in past generations.

When I first told my grandmother I was gay, she had a difficult time understanding why I couldn't just keep it a secret. She said, "I understand that this is how it is and that you're not going to change, but why do you have to tell anyone?" At first, my grandmother didn't understand that it's not like keeping a secret about a surprise party, although she did eventually accept my wish to be open about my sexual orientation and came to love my partner like a grandson (she called him her grandson).

Because your sexual orientation involves many aspects of your life, especially when you get older and begin having relationships, you often wind up having to answer questions with a lie if you want to keep it a secret. People ask questions all the time, such as: "Do you have a boyfriend?" "Do you have a girlfriend?" "Are you married?" So keeping your sexual orientation a secret becomes a huge job, because you can never say anything that might reveal the truth, even if you have to lie and make up stories. And that can make a person feel very alone, as if nobody knows who they really are. (It can also make some gay young people act in ways you wouldn't expect, like calling other gay people names—or even physically attacking them—to deflect suspicions anyone might have about their sexuality.)

We don't ask straight people to keep their feelings secret, because we think that the love between males and females is a great thing. I think the same should be true for gay people—loving someone of the same sex is a perfectly natural thing for gay people and it doesn't hurt anyone, so why hide it?

✱ Why do some gay people keep their sexual orientation a secret or pretend that they're straight?

There are many reasons: They don't want to risk getting teased or beaten up at school; they don't want to risk being rejected by their friends and families; they feel bad or embarrassed about being gay; they want to fit in; they have anti-gay religious beliefs; they don't want people to look down on them; and they want to avoid discrimination at work.

Jake, the seventeen-year-old high school student who has been attracted to guys since kindergarten, is afraid that if his friends and family know the truth, they'll look down on him. To make sure they don't find out, he's dating a girl at school. "Having a girlfriend means they won't think I'm gay. It's tough, because my girlfriend expects me to have sex with her, but I can't imagine doing it."

Mae is eighteen and lives in a small town about an hour from Atlanta. While she's told all of her classmates and her mother that she's gay, she hasn't brought up the subject with her father or stepmother because she's afraid of how they'll react. "My stepmom is really religious, and my dad has become that way. I'm putting it off for now. But I'll probably tell them in the near future. I've been debating about how to tell him."

When Mark was growing up on eastern Long Island, he thought he would have to keep his sexual orientation a secret forever because of what he heard at his Pentecostal church. "I remember sitting in church feeling very nervous, because every other week, from out of nowhere, the pastor would list the sins of the world: abortion, homosexuality, and Democrats. To be honest, I thought I was going to hell. I thought everyone would hate me if they ever found out."

❈ What is homophobia?

"Homophobia" means fear or hatred of gay people. Although it's natural to feel confused by homosexuality, being mean or hateful toward someone who is gay is no different from being mean or hateful toward someone of a different race or religion than you—it's prejudice, and it's wrong.

People often feel uncomfortable with the whole subject of homosexuality and gay people, especially if they've never met someone who is gay. (I felt plenty uncomfortable with the whole thing when I was a teenager and *I'm* gay!) Some people have very negative feelings about homosexuality, and meeting someone who is gay doesn't change that—they may act in hateful ways toward gay people, calling them names or worse. But for many people, those feelings go away as soon as they get to know someone who is gay.

❈ Why do some people call other people "fag" or "faggot" or "dyke" or say things like "Don't be so gay" or "That's so gay"?

A lot of young people don't know exactly what these words mean, but they use them as curse words and put-downs. They know that when they say "That's so gay," what they're saying is, "That's dumb, that's stupid." They may not realize that their words are offensive and hurtful to gay people in the same way they would be to Jewish people if they said "That's so Jewish" in the context of a put-down.

The word "faggot" has long been a slur word used against men and boys who were thought to be weak and sensitive. They weren't necessarily gay, but they weren't masculine in the way many people think men should be. Today, "fag" and "faggot" are still used as slurs against gay men, as well as men and boys who are simply not considered masculine, regardless of their sexual orientation. "Fag" is also used more generally as a slur word, as in "Stop joking around, you're being such a fag." "Dyke" is a similar word used to describe a lesbian, or a girl or woman who is masculine or aggressive.

The word "gay" was adopted in the late 1960s and early 1970s by a new generation of gay rights activists, who preferred it over the more clinical-sounding "homosexual" or "homophile." It wasn't until recent years that the word "gay" has come to be used as a slur or curse word among young people.

Some gay people may call their friends "fag" and "dyke" in a playful way. If you're straight, keep in mind that the gay people you know may not like these words, or may only be comfortable hearing them from other gay people, who they can trust aren't using them to be hurtful. I think it's a big mistake for anyone to use these words, because to me they're hurtful no matter who is saying them, no matter what the context.

✳ I've heard that sometimes the people doing the name-calling may be gay or confused about their own sexuality. Why would someone do that?

At summer camp, when I was fourteen, a girl I didn't want to date decided to get back at me by telling my bunkmates that I was a fag. From then on, my bunkmates, as well as some of the other kids at camp, called me "fag" or "faggot." Years later, I learned that one of my bunkmates was also gay. He wasn't the one who initiated the name-calling, but he went along with it. And even though I never had the opportunity to ask him, I'm guessing he joined in the name-calling to avoid bringing attention to himself—and I'm also guessing that he was relieved that he wasn't the one being called names.

So some kids who are gay might call other people names to avoid the possibility that anyone will think *they* are gay. Others initiate the name-calling—or worse—in an attempt to prove that they're straight, even if underneath they're conflicted about their sexuality or already know they're gay. And sometimes the name-calling comes from people who are straight, but feeling confused and uncomfortable with their feelings of same-sex attraction. It's perfectly natural for all people, particularly adolescents, to have feelings of same-sex attraction, whether or not those attractions wind up being intense and/or lasting. But there's no reason to use that discomfort to attack others.

If you asked a psychologist to explain this kind of behavior (which I did), this is what she might say: Young people who are conflicted about their sexuality and/or have negative feelings about being gay sometimes lash out at other gay people as a way of trying to beat down or deny the part of themselves that they feel bad about or hate.

✳ What does "queer" mean? Is it a slur?

When I was growing up, you called a kid "queer" if you thought he was gay; "queer" was used as a slur, like "fag." Some gay people also used "queer" in a playful way among themselves.

In the 1990s a new generation of gay young people started using "queer" as a substitute for "gay" or "lesbian." They didn't see "queer" as a slur anymore, but instead embraced it as an inclusive word that took in all kinds of people, including gay men, lesbians, bisexuals, transgender people, and anyone else who was considered outside the mainstream. For example, when Molly was coming to terms with her sexuality, she realized, "You don't need definitions or labels. You are who you are. You don't need to call it anything. That's when I embraced the term 'queer.'"

"Queer" also came to be used in college and university programs, as in "queer studies." Despite the new use of this word, there are many gay people who still find it offensive.

If you have a friend who is gay and you're not sure which words she's comfortable with, you can ask, or you can pay attention to the words she uses to describe herself and her gay friends. For every person who happily calls himself queer, there's another person who finds that word hurtful.

✳ What is it like when people care about someone gay—such as a friend or relative— and they hear anti-gay language?

For people who know and care about a person who is gay, hearing someone use anti-gay slurs can make them feel uncomfortable, upset, angry, frightened, or hurt. And it also puts them in the often difficult position of trying to figure out what, if anything, to say in response.

Erica is in the sixth grade at a private school in Maryland and she has an uncle who is gay. Every day at school she hears kids call one another "faggot" and use put-downs like "That's so gay." She told me: "It makes me really, really uncomfortable, and I'll give them that look that says, 'Stop it, it's not nice to make fun of these people.' But I'm afraid to say something direct. It makes me scared. A lot of times it's hard to stand up for what you think, because you feel outnumbered."

Chris Lord, one of Erica's teachers, has made no secret of the fact that his father is gay and that he has no patience for anti-gay language. "My father and mother split when I was very young and I didn't meet my father until five years ago, which is when I first found out he was gay. But it wasn't an issue for me. My mom always had gay friends. When I was very young, I didn't really understand what it meant to be gay, but it became something natural to me. So from an early age I had a problem with those words. It still makes me cringe when I hear them."

✳ What's it like for people who are gay or lesbian when they hear someone use the word "fag" or hear someone say "That's so gay"?

It hurts when you hear people say these things, especially if you hear it from friends or family. But it can also make you angry, and if the words are meant for you, it can feel very threatening and scary.

Mae was in ninth grade when her classmates started calling her names. "My girlfriend and I had just broken up. She wanted to get back at me, so even though our relationship had been a secret, she told everyone I was gay. Just walking down the hall, people called me a dyke and a lesbo. These were people who had been my friends and decided not to be anymore, and people I didn't even know, but they'd heard I was gay. It hurt. And it made me angry. Anyone calling you a name is going to make you angry."

Kevin, who is gay and attends high school in southern California, is the president of his school's GSA (Gay-Straight Alliance). He's very open about being gay, and is routinely called names by a handful of students. "Under their breath they'll say, 'faggot.' They never do it in an obvious way, because at my high school, if someone yelled out 'faggot' at another student, they'd be shunned." Kevin says that he doesn't let it bother him because he knows he'll have a good life no matter what these students say.

Besides the under-the-breath name-calling, Kevin said that people at his school also routinely say "fag" and "gay" as slurs, but it's not directed at anyone in particular and he doesn't let that bother him either. "I take it with a grain of salt because most of them don't know what they're saying. Most kids are pretty smart and if they knew that what they were saying was hurting people, they wouldn't say it."

On the other hand, a lot of people *do* know what they're saying, or at least they know that using these words will be hurtful. As an adult, because of my work, I've been called "faggot" every now and then by adults. It still makes me cringe—it's a reflex—but that kind of language doesn't hurt me as it did when I was young. Mostly, now, it just makes me sad, because I'd hoped that by now, people would know better. Unfortunately, prejudice in all its ugly forms is still alive and well here in the United States and around the world.

✷ If you hear someone using anti-gay language or if someone calls you "faggot" or "dyke," should you say anything?

For young people, I have only one rule when it comes to saying something in response to people who use the word "gay" as a slur or who use other anti-gay language: You should never say anything if you think that saying it could put you in some sort of danger. Also, if you are gay, by challenging someone's remarks you might bring unwanted attention to yourself, especially if you don't want anyone to think you're gay.

Of course, each situation is different, and even if there doesn't seem to be any danger in challenging someone, it can be very scary to stand up on your own and say what you think. (Even at my age, I still find it difficult to challenge people who make negative remarks about gay people.) But if you find yourself in a position to say something, you can simply respond by saying, "I don't like hearing those words, I find them offensive, and they're hurtful to people who are gay."

When it comes to teachers and parents, I think it's absolutely their responsibility to make clear that anti-gay language—and any other kind of slur—is wrong and that it shouldn't be used by anyone at any time. Unfortunately, teachers and parents can sometimes be prejudiced, or afraid, or simply might not know what to say. (For more on why teachers might be afraid, see Chapter 6, "School.")

I wish all parents and teachers could be as confident and clear as one of my college friends. When she recently heard her nine-year-old son call his younger brother a "faggot," she knew he didn't understand what he was saying. So she sat him down and offered this simple, but firm explanation: "I said that 'faggot' was a mean word for someone who was gay, and that 'gay' was a word used to describe two people of the same sex who love each other in the same way that his dad and I love each other." My friend also told her son that some people love someone of the same sex, instead of the opposite sex, and that she had friends who were gay. She went on to explain "that these words hurt their feelings a lot and I didn't use these words and didn't like them. I said that I love my friends and I didn't want them to be hurt and that 'gay' wasn't a bad word but people sometimes used it in a mean way. My son doesn't like to hurt anyone's feelings, so I think he understood."

chapter 2
friends and family

N ow that you know the basics, you might be thinking about how to talk to your friends and family about sexual orientation. Whether you think a friend or relative might be gay and want to help him or her open up to you, or you're struggling with how to tell the people close to you that you're gay, this can feel like a difficult subject to discuss. It might be hard to find the courage to bring it up and it's not easy to figure out what kind of response you'll get when you do. I hope this chapter will help begin the discussion and bring greater understanding when it comes to gay friends and relatives.

✳ If I think my friend is gay, can I ask him/her about it? What should I say?

Most of the time I'm asked this question by someone who is concerned about a friend and his or her friendship with that person. She senses there's something going on that's creating distance between her and her friend and she'd like to get things out in the open so they can be better friends. Or she's worried that a friend is struggling with conflicts about his or her sexuality and she'd like to let that friend know that it's okay to talk about it.

So if this is your motivation, yes, you can ask. But before you do, keep in mind that if your friend is gay, he or she may be afraid to answer honestly, especially if your friend is unsure about how you feel about gay people. If he has been keeping his sexual orientation a secret, he might also be afraid that you won't keep his secret for him. So, in asking, you need to make sure he knows that you are asking out of concern and that you can be trusted. For example, you can say, "You're my friend. I care about you and really want to understand you. I've been wondering if you might be gay. I could be totally off base here, but I want you to know that if you are, I'm okay with that and you can trust me not to tell anyone if you don't want me to."

Depending on his circumstances, your friend could respond in a number of different ways. If, for example, he says yes, that he's gay, then that can be the beginning of a much longer conversation and a better friendship. If he isn't gay, he'll tell you he's not. And because some people think that being gay is a bad thing, he might be upset that you would think he was. If he doesn't yet have a full under-standing of his feelings, he might say that he isn't gay or that he's unsure. And even if he is gay and knows it, he may still not be comfortable telling you. That's what hap-pened with Mae and her best friend.

In ninth grade, when Mae's best friend asked her if she was gay, she said that she wasn't, that the things kids had been saying at school were just rumors. Mae told me: "I was scared of her reaction. She said it didn't matter either way, but regardless of what she said, I was still afraid that it might change something. Me and her were good friends and I didn't want that to change." But Mae took comfort in thinking that her friend was someone she might be able to talk to one day.

✱ I'm afraid to ask my friend directly. What else can I do to let my friend know he can talk to me?

If you're not comfortable being really direct, you can indicate to your friend that you're okay with gay people by talking positively about someone you know who is gay and open about it. You might also talk about a television show that has a gay character, or you can bring up some other cultural reference. By letting your friend know that you are comfortable with the subject, you might give him the room he needs to feel comfortable enough to talk to you about himself.

✳ How do you get up the courage to ask?

First you need to think about why you're scared. Are you afraid that your friend will be mad if you ask? Are you afraid that you could be wrong? Are you afraid that you'll hurt your friendship if you're wrong?

In the worst case, which isn't really so bad, you could be wrong and your friend might get mad. But if you're right, then by asking, you've given your friend an opportunity to talk about what he or she is feeling, and that will make you better friends. A lot of times, gay people are afraid of how their friends will react if they tell the truth, so they hesitate to say anything unless someone asks them.

It's perfectly normal to be afraid of the unknown. That's a good reason to be careful and to think about what to say, but that's not a good reason to give up on trying to be a good friend.

✳ I think my best friend is gay/lesbian. Will he/she want to have sex with me?

One of the myths about gay people is that they're sexually attracted to everyone of the same sex. The truth is, gay people are like straight people in that they're sexually attracted only to some people, but not most. You probably don't worry about your straight friends of the opposite sex wanting to hook up with you, and just the same, there is no reason to worry that your gay friends will want to hook up with you. And, in any case, if any friend wants to be with you sexually and you don't want to, all you have to do is tell him or her that you're not interested.

✳ I have a friend who is gay and very upset about it. My friend has talked about committing suicide. What should I do?

You should take what your friend says as seriously as you would any friend who talks about committing suicide. The first thing to do is encourage your friend to talk to an adult. If he can't or won't do that, then you need to get immediate help for him. This is not something you can be responsible for on your own, and you must talk to an adult—a teacher, school counselor or nurse, or a parent—and tell her that you have a friend who has talked about committing suicide. If your friend has confided in you that he is gay, you can still get help for him without telling anyone about his sexual orientation. If you don't feel comfortable talking to any of the adults you know, call a local suicide hotline (look in your phone book, call infor-mation, or search online), or call 1-800-SUICIDE. You can find more resources in Chapter 9, "Resources."

✳ I'm gay and I'd like to tell my friends, but I'm afraid to. What should I do?

It's perfectly natural to want to tell your friends that you're gay. Not telling them means keeping a big secret about yourself and maybe even having to pretend that you're not gay. It's also perfectly natural to be afraid of saying anything. Some people have negative feelings about homosexuality, so it's scary to bring up the subject with people who are important to you, especially if you don't know how they might react. Will they still want to be your friend? Will they look down on you? Will they be supportive? Will they be scared?

Jennifer, who is gay and is now in her second year of college, came out to all of her friends after she graduated from high school. But, she said, "You should be cautious about the people you tell. Before I told anyone I was gay, I said to them, 'How judgmental are you?' And if they said, 'Not very,' I then asked, 'Will you love me no matter what?' And if they said, 'Yes,' then I told them I was gay. I've never had one person say, 'I can't be your friend' because of it."

Kevin, who is open about being gay at his southern California high school, suggested that you think about your friends' attitudes before telling them that you're gay. He said: "Test the waters. Kids will generally know if their friends are accepting."

You can test the waters by bringing up the subject

without talking about yourself. Talk about something you saw on television or, if you have a gay relative, talk about him or her. If your friend responds with very strong negative feelings, he will probably have difficulty with the news that you're gay. If, however, your friend is open and supportive of gay people, or just neutral, then you know that this is a friend you can probably talk to.

Mae, who is now a high school senior, has told all of her friends that she's gay, and most of her classmates at school know as well. She offered this final note of caution: "When you come out, there's always going to be somebody who doesn't agree with it or somebody who hurts your feelings. So you have to be strong enough to handle that."

If you don't think you're strong enough yet, the best thing to do is wait until you feel that you are. You'll know when the time is right.

✳ How do people react when they find out a friend is gay?

Good friends should be supportive and understanding, which is how fourteen-year-old Tony's friends reacted when he first talked to them. He wrote to me: "My friends were all really cool when I told 'em I was gay, but they already knew. Now we talk about guys and stuff all the time. (Oh, yeah, all of my friends were straight girls at the time.)"

But not everyone is instantly supportive and understanding. If people are prejudiced or have strict religious beliefs, they may not want to be friends once they discover that their friend is gay. That's what happened to Mae when she was in ninth grade. Her friends heard rumors that she was gay and most of them avoided her. She recalled, "People who I thought were my friends didn't want to have anything to do with me, just because of that."

Two of Mae's friends, Misty and Kendall, stuck by her, but because she was afraid of how they might react, she told them that the rumors weren't true. A year later, when Mae told Misty she was gay, Misty got mad. "She was mad because I didn't come out and tell her the truth in the first place. She told me that she thought we were better friends than that. I didn't trust that she was telling the truth when she said it would be okay with her if I was gay, but I should have. After she got over being mad, everything was fine."

Friends can also react with surprise or confusion, especially if they never considered the possibility that their friend could be gay. That's what happened to Howard when his best buddy came out to him during their freshman year of college. "I was shocked. Maybe I'm stupid or something, but we'd been friends for nearly a whole year and, like, I didn't have a clue. I always thought you could tell if a guy was gay, and it never occurred to me, especially since we always talked about girls." Howard said that after his friend came out to him, their friendship was never the same. "I didn't trust him to tell me the truth after that. I felt really betrayed."

But more often than not, good friends do their best to be understanding and may even be curious about what it's like to be gay. Caroline, who is sixteen, and plays on her high school's tennis team in south Florida, has confided in only a couple of her friends after they asked her directly if she was gay. She said, "At first I tried to give the impression that I wasn't, because I was so scared they would hate me. But then I started crying and told them the truth. They were my friends. I couldn't lie to them. And it turned out that they were great. They didn't think it was any big deal. Now they think I'm some sort of expert and they ask me questions all the time because they want to know what it's like for me to be a lesbian."

Cynthia tried hard to be understanding with a friend she thought was gay, but he wasn't very cooperative when she tried talking to him about it. "We'd been friends since first grade. He really liked girls and hung out with a group of us all through junior high school. It was like he was one of us. I even asked him a few times if he was gay, but he always got mad when I asked, so I just waited for him to tell me. It took him a long time, but finally during senior year he had a boyfriend, so it was kind of stupid not to tell me, so he did." Cynthia asked her friend why he hadn't told her before and he explained that he was afraid of how she would react. She said, "That was so lame. He knew it was no big deal for me. I still don't understand what his problem was, but now we talk about everything. We're better friends."

✳ I have a crush on my friend (not a platonic crush, but the kind of crush where I want a romantic relationship). Can I tell him/her?

Maybe. But before you say anything, you have to think about this carefully. First, whether you're gay or straight, there is always the risk that your friend will not have the same feelings for you, so you have to be prepared for that possibility.

Second, if you happen to be gay or lesbian, there are a few other risks to consider, depending upon your situation. For example, I recently received an e-mail from Steven, who attends a middle school in a small Southern city. He wrote: "I have a new friend who moved here a few months ago. I like him a lot and we spend a lot of time together and I think I have a crush on him. I don't think he knows I'm gay and I don't know if he's gay. I want to tell him how I feel, but I'm afraid he won't feel the same way."

As I learned from later e-mails, Steven has not yet told his parents that he's gay and has not told anyone at school, either. He doesn't plan to tell his parents until he's older because he's heard them say that homosexuality is wrong. He also thinks it would be a really bad idea for anyone at school to find out he's gay. And he doesn't know his friend's attitude toward gay people, although he's never heard him say anything negative.

So here is the worst-case scenario if Steven decides to tell his friend about his crush on him: His friend could reject him and then decide to tell other kids at school that Steven is gay. The friend might also tell his parents that Steven is gay, and they might then contact Steven's parents.

I suggested to Steven that, given his situation, it was not a good idea to share his feelings with his friend right away. But I also suggested that he could find out more about his friend's attitudes, and if his friend turned out to be supportive and was trustworthy, he might eventually decide to come out to his friend. And if it turned out that his friend was also gay, and could be trusted, then Steven could consider telling his friend about his crush.

When you get older and you no longer live at home and have to worry about what your parents and/or classmates think, it's far less risky to tell someone you have a crush on them. But even when you're an adult, you still face the risk that the person you have a crush on won't feel the same way about you, and that can hurt whether you're gay or straight.

✳ My friend who is gay told me she's fallen in love with me. What should I say?

If you like your friend in the same way, then you can tell her how you feel. If you don't feel the same as she does, then tell her that you're sorry, but you don't have the same feelings. It may feel awkward to be that direct, but that's often the best way. If you're still comfortable being friends with her, you can reassure her of that as well. And, it goes without saying, it's important to respect your friend's privacy and not tell everyone you know that she's in love with you.

✳ I'm not gay, but I like hanging out with my gay friends. Is there something wrong with me?

There is absolutely nothing wrong with you. Many straight people have gay friends. And many gay people have straight friends.

✳ Can I ask my gay friends questions about what it's like to be gay?

Yes, you can ask, and as long as your questions are respectful and show a real desire to understand, most gay and lesbian people will be happy to answer. But keep in mind that not every gay person is comfortable talking about being gay or has the answers to your specific questions. In addition, your friend can only speak for him- or herself. Like straight people, gay people have a variety of experiences and opinions. So it's also a good idea to do a little independent research of your own, like reading this book and other books or checking out some of the websites I recommend.

I've been surprised by how rarely my straight friends have asked me questions about being gay. I've written several books about gay people, so they know I'm not shy about the subject. Finally, I asked some of my friends why they haven't asked me questions. Most told me that they were afraid to say something that might hurt my feelings and they didn't want me to think they were stupid. But like I said in the introduction, the only stupid question is the one you don't ask.

Some gay people don't like answering questions because they feel straight people should know everything already. But I think we have an obligation to help others understand what it's like to be a gay person. If gay people don't do this, who will?

✳ I'm gay. How can I become friends with other young people who are gay and lesbian?

This is the one question I'm asked in e-mails more than any other by people who feel very isolated and lonely.

I remember being really frustrated when I was in my teens because I never met anyone gay who was my age. I had one gay friend, but he was twenty-three and I had a crush on him so I couldn't talk to him like he was one of my buddies (I was so attracted to him that I could hardly look at him without turning red). It wasn't until I got to college that I met lots of gay people my own age.

Gay people come out earlier now than when I was young, so there are more opportunities for gay teens to meet one another. There's also the advantage of the Internet, where you can meet young gay people all over the country on sites like www.youthresource.com. (For more sites and for more information about being safe when meeting people online, see Chapter 9, "Resources.")

If you go to a school that has a GSA (Gay-Straight Alliance) or if there is a gay and lesbian youth group in your community, then you're in luck because you can find people to talk to who are your own age. But I know that even if there's a gay youth group nearby, you may not want anyone in your community to know that you're gay, so that could keep you from going. Or it may not be so easy to get to the community center where the gay youth group meets, especially if you're too young to drive and/or don't want your parents to know what you're doing.

That was the problem for one girl who wrote to me about how she travels by bus from her small town to a nearby city to attend a weekly gay youth support group. She hates to lie to her parents, but she told them that she was volunteering at a center for senior citizens. "I know I'm taking a chance, but it's a risk I have to take," she wrote. "There's no one at my school I can talk to and my parents are very religious, so I can't talk to them."

If, like most young people, you don't have a GSA at your school or a local gay and lesbian youth group, you could be the pioneer who starts one. For more information on starting a GSA, check out the Gay-Straight Alliance Network (www.gsanetwork.org).

Sometimes I get e-mails from kids as young as ten and eleven who feel isolated because there are very, very few people their age who are gay and out. My advice to them is to find a way to talk to their parents if they can, or else to find a family friend, relative, or school counselor to talk to. It's very difficult when you feel completely alone with your thoughts and feelings, so even if you can't find someone your own age, you can at least find someone who is understanding and a good listener.

✳ How do parents react when they find out a child is lesbian or gay?

Some parents are immediately understanding and loving, while others react with confusion, sadness, denial, guilt, embarrassment, tears, or anger. Some parents even reject their children, going so far as to throw them out of the house, though this is the exception.

More typically, parents may wonder what they did wrong, they may express concern about AIDS (more on this in Chapter 4, "Sex"), they may be upset that a child has not talked to them sooner, and they may hope that this is just a phase, especially if their child is still young. All too often their reactions are based on the myths and stereotypes they grew up with and not on the truth about what it means to be gay or lesbian.

For parents who have strict religious beliefs, the discovery that a child is gay or lesbian can be especially difficult. These parents will likely find themselves torn between what their religion tells them about homosexuality and their love for their child. (Please see Chapter 5, "God and Religion," for more on this topic.)

My own mother's reaction was pretty average. She didn't cry or feel guilty, but she was disappointed, sad, worried, and confused, which left me feeling pretty awful. No one likes to disappoint his mother. She also didn't want me to tell anyone, because she was afraid of what people would think. In remembering the experience many years later, she said, "I felt that if anyone knew, then my son would be stigmatized, rejected, looked at as defective or inferior. Somehow I couldn't bear the thought of someone judging him."

Like most parents, my mother eventually got used to me being gay. But my mom went well beyond getting used to having a gay son and became politically active in the gay civil rights effort through an organization for parents of gay people called Parents, Families and Friends of Lesbians and Gays (PFLAG). And, later in life, once I had a partner, my mom always treated him like he was another son.

These days, because people know a lot more about homosexuality and have friends and family members who are openly gay, there are more and more parents who have thought about the possibility of a child being gay and are prepared if the subject comes up.

That was the case with Jennifer, who told her mother she was gay when she was nineteen. Jennifer recalled, "My mother was fine. She said she had known since I was twelve. One of her friends told her he thought I was gay. Looking back, I can remember my mother saying things like she knew. With my sister, she would say 'when you bring your husband home.' With me, she would always say 'when you bring a person home.'"

✳ If I think I'm gay, can I tell my parents?

If you've thought very seriously about how they will respond and feel certain that they will be comfortable with the news that you're gay, then you should consider talking to your parents. Ideally, the more open you can be with your parents, the better your relationship with them will be.

But before you do anything, you need to think very carefully about how your parents are likely to react. Not all parents are loving and supportive of their gay children. Some parents can react very badly to the news that a child is gay. Some have even completely rejected their gay children and forced them to leave home. Others have sent their children away to special programs that are designed to "turn" gay kids into straight kids. While these cases are generally the exception, you still need a very good idea of how your parents will react before you say anything.

If there is any reason for you to think that your parents

62

will react badly, then the best thing to do is to find other people to talk to now and wait until you're older and no longer dependent on your parents before talking to them.

✳ How can I figure out how my parents will react if I tell them I'm gay?

You can never be absolutely certain how a parent will react, but you can get a pretty good idea of whether your parents will react with understanding and concern or with anger and hostility. If your parents are the kind of people you talk to about everything, and they have talked positively in the past about gay issues and gay people, then you can expect your parents will come to accept what you tell them.

If, however, your parents hold strict religious beliefs against homosexuality or have expressed negative opinions about gay people, you can expect that they will have a very difficult time and may never come to terms with what you tell them. And even if they are accepting of gay people in general, they may have a difficult time hearing that their child is gay. They could mistakenly see it as a negative reflection on their parenting skills, or they may feel your life will be more difficult than if you were straight. (And they would be right about your life being more difficult: Being gay means you will probably encounter prejudice or discrimination at some point in your life.) No matter how understanding they are, your parents are people, too, and may need time to adjust to this news.

Kevin, who is in high school and lives with his mother, has what I think is a good plan of action for trying to figure out what your parents think and how they might react. He told me: "You need to scope them out. Let's say you're watching TV with your mom and dad, and there's a gay interest story or news story. Ask them what they think. Or just bring up that you have a gay friend and maybe talk about how he's having a problem with his parents and what do they think of that."

When it came to talking to his own mother, Kevin said, "I just knew she was neutral about it. For one thing, we're not highly religious people. The last time my mom and I went to church together was probably five years ago. That was the first clue I had that she didn't have an opinion either way." Still, when Kevin told his mom, she cried for three days before letting him know she was okay with what he'd told her. Based on that experience, Kevin added, "If you come out, give your parents time and eventually they'll come around to it. In my case, it was three days; in someone else's, it might be thirty years." (For more information on coming out to parents, including some books that I recommend, see Chapter 9, "Resources.")

✳ If I think I'm gay, but I can't talk to my own parents, are there other parents I can talk to?

Yes, absolutely. There are many thousands of parents across the country who are members of Parents, Families and Friends of Lesbians and Gays (PFLAG). Most members are parents who have gay and lesbian children themselves. If you contact your local chapter, you'll find an accepting mom or dad who has lots of experience with these issues. They will be more than happy to talk to you in confidence (see Chapter 9, "Resources," for contact information).

✳ If one of my close relatives, like my sister or father or uncle, is gay, does that mean I'll be gay too?

No. Even if a close relative is gay, the odds are that you will be straight.

✳ But isn't there a genetic component to being gay?

Yes, there is. Studies of twins indicate that there is a significant genetic component when it comes to sexual orientation, but sexual orientation isn't exclusively determined by our genes. If it were, identical twins would always both be straight or both be gay (identical twins have exactly the same genes because they come from the same fertilized egg). But it turns out that when one twin is gay, there is a 50-50 possibility the other twin will be gay. And scientists who study these things are still sorting out why (if you're thinking of becoming a scientist, this is one area of research where there's still a lot to learn).

So while there *is* a genetic component to sexual orientation, it is only one factor that goes into which gender you're attracted to. That means that unless you're an identical twin and your twin is gay, it's safe to say that the odds are your chances of being gay are no different from that of the average person with or without a gay relative. That said, my answer is something of an oversimplification. If you're really curious about this, I suggest doing some of your own research to see what scientists studying this subject are saying. (I recommend starting with the work of research scientists J. M. Bailey and R. C. Pillard.)

✳ Will my gay friends or relatives try to make me gay?

No. And even if someone tried to make you gay, he or she couldn't. No one can make you gay, just as no one can make you straight.

✳ My aunt Sharon and aunt Sonya are a lesbian couple, but I've never seen them touch each other or hold hands. Why not?

This question reminds me of one my mother asked me many years ago, when I had my first boyfriend after college. She said, "You're never affectionate with each other. Is there some sort of problem between the two of you?"

My mother's question surprised me because when Billy

66

and I were alone or with our friends, we acted like any other couple. But when we were with my mother or out in public, we never held hands or kissed each other hello and good-bye. That was because we grew up in the 1970s, a time when our being affectionate in public would have been a problem for a lot of people. They might have stared at us, called us names, or even tried to hurt us (which is still sometimes the case in a lot of places).

With my mother, I was afraid that she would be uncomfortable, which would have made *me* uncomfortable, so my boyfriend and I just acted like we were a couple of straight guys hanging out with each other. It wasn't like we had to try very hard. For us, it was automatic.

When I explained to my mother why Billy and I weren't affectionate in front of her, she said, "Well, I hope you'll feel free to be yourselves when you're around me. That would make me very happy."

It took a while, but over time I learned to be myself, so now my partner and I act like any other married couple. That doesn't mean we dance together at every wedding or hold hands when we're walking down the street. While times have changed and gay people are more open than they were in the past and generally have less to worry about in terms of their personal safety, plenty of gay and lesbian couples are often reluctant to be themselves in public situations, including at family events like weddings.

For example, several years ago, my cousin Rob had a huge wedding and my partner and I were the only gay couple there. During the wedding reception, when the dance floor was packed, my cousin Bernice came over to our table and told us she hoped we felt comfortable enough to dance like everyone else.

We thanked my cousin for the encouragement—it was really thoughtful of her—but Barney and I never danced that night. I'm sure no one would have said anything, but we were feeling a little shy. No same-sex couple had ever danced together at a Marcus family event, and we just didn't feel comfortable drawing that much attention to ourselves.

The day after the family wedding, we attended the small wedding of my best buddy and his bride. My partner and I felt completely comfortable at that celebration, which included several other gay and lesbian people, so the two of us rarely left the dance floor. No one stared at us. No one commented. We all had a great time. And we had a blast being ourselves. My mother would have been proud of us.

These days, straight people are more used to being around out gay people, so my partner and I, like a lot of other gay men and lesbians, find it easier to be ourselves. Also, now that we're older, we don't worry as much about what people think. Still, we're careful to consider where we are if we choose to do anything that would indicate we're a couple, like holding hands, giving each other a kiss hello or good-bye, or dancing together at a public event. However much things have changed, there are still people who have very negative feelings about gay men and lesbians and sometimes these people use words and/or their fists to express themselves. As my partner and I see it, there's no point in risking our safety just to demonstrate that we love each other. We know that already. And there's no reason for you to risk your personal safety either.

✳ My parents are divorced and I think it may be because one of them is gay. Is it okay to ask?

You can ask, but that doesn't mean your parents will give you a direct answer. If, in fact, your mother or father is gay, your parents themselves may be having difficulty dealing with the situation and may not want to talk about it. They may also consider it a private matter between the two of them. They may think you are too young to discuss it. Your gay parent may fear being rejected by you. Or your parents may fear that talking with you will upset or burden you.

Some parents, however, are relieved to be asked. I remember one divorced friend whose eight- and ten-year-old sons asked one day over breakfast, "Mom, are you gay?" My friend was startled at first, because she didn't think her boys had any idea. "You can fool yourself into thinking that your kids don't know what's going on, but they knew and they were looking for confirmation. I thought it was only fair to tell them the truth." My friend had been afraid to tell her sons because she was scared of how they might react, but as she explained to me, "They didn't really care. They just wanted to be sure that I loved them. And, of course, I do. I'm so glad the whole thing is out in the open now and it's a non-issue."

✳ I live with my two moms. Why won't some of my friends' parents let their kids come to my house?

Some people are still very uninformed about gay men and lesbians and they think that if their kids get to know gay people, it will somehow make their children gay. Others mistakenly believe that gay men and women are more likely to molest their children. And still others think that being gay is wrong or sinful and don't want their children exposed to such "bad influences."

✳ I have a gay parent and I'd like to talk to other kids who are in the same boat. How do I find them?

There is an organization for people who have gay parents. It's called Children of Lesbians & Gays Everywhere (COLAGE). See Chapter 9, "Resources," for contact information.

chapter 3
dating, marriage, and kids

A lot of what I write about in this chapter may seem pretty obvious, especially because in most ways, gay and lesbian people are just like straight people when it comes to their personal lives: They date, they have relationships, they make lifelong commitments to the person they love and, these days, more and more are having kids. Gay people may face more challenges when it comes to building family life, but in general, gay women and men want the same things out of life that straight people do: companionship and love.

✳ What do gay people do on a date?

When gay people go on dates, they do the same things

straight people do, except you're not as likely to see male or female couples holding hands or kissing in public.

✳ Why don't gay people hold hands and kiss in public?

If there were no prejudice and gay and lesbian people were safe from discrimination and harassment, you would see gay and lesbian couples on dates holding hands or kissing in public, just like straight couples. But that's not the case, so the places where you're most likely to see gay and lesbian couples being affectionate in public are those where they feel safe. This includes neighborhoods where many gay and lesbian people live, popular gay and lesbian resorts like Provincetown, Massachusetts, gay clubs and restaurants, and public events such as gay pride parades and festivals.

✳ If two people of the same sex go on a date, who does the asking? Who pays?

Traditionally, for straight people, boys ask girls out and boys are expected to pay the expenses. That's no longer the hard-and-fast rule it was when my parents and grandparents were dating, but many straight people still fall back on that tradition. For gay and lesbian people, that's not a tradition they can depend on, for obvious reasons. But if the date is going to happen, someone has to do the asking, and someone has to pay.

Without clearly defined roles based on who is the "boy" and who is the "girl," gay and lesbian people are relatively free to do what they want (this is one advantage of being gay). So the person who does the asking is usually the one who feels more strongly about wanting to go on the date, or is more comfortable doing the asking, or is less afraid of being rejected. And when it comes to who pays, there are also choices. The person who did the asking may want to pay, or the person who is more comfortable spending money, or the couple may just split the bill.

✳ Are gay men attracted to all men? Are lesbians attracted to all women?

No, but some people believe that gay men are attracted to every man, teenager, and boy they see. And they imagine that lesbians are attracted to every woman, teenager, and girl they see. That is just as foolish as believing that straight men and women are attracted to every person of the opposite sex. Sexual feelings of attraction are complex and selective, which means you will be attracted to some people, but not most. And even if someone has feelings of attraction for another person, most often the circumstances aren't appropriate for them to act on those feelings, so they don't.

73

✳ If a gay guy or a lesbian asks me out, what should I do?

Before you say anything, put yourself in the other person's shoes and imagine what it was like for him or her to get up the courage to ask you out in the first place. With this in mind, whatever you say, remember to be kind. If you're not interested, you can simply say, thank you, but I'm not interested. If you *are* interested, then you're in luck!

Sometimes straight people react strongly when someone mistakenly assumes that they are gay. They get upset that anyone could think that they're gay, because they think being gay is something bad. But since being gay isn't bad, there is no reason to feel insulted or to get upset. If a gay person asks you out on a date, whether or not you want to go, think of it as a compliment.

✳ Do gay people fall in love?

Just like everyone else, gay and lesbian people fall in love.

✳ When gay people have a relationship, is one the husband and one the wife? Is it different from how my parents are?

Gay and lesbian people have couple relationships that are as varied as the couple relationships straight people have. Some are like traditional marriages from my grandparents' generation, where one partner goes to work and the other

74

stays home. But most gay and lesbian couples are like most straight couples: Both partners work, both contribute in different ways to taking care of the various household chores and responsibilities, and both share in decision making.

✳ Do gay people want to get married? Why?

Of course most gay people want to get married, just like most straight people want to get married. And they want to do so because they fall in love, make commitments to each other, and want to take care of each other (and their children, if they have any) in the same way that straight married people do.

Like other people, gay men and lesbians want the practical and emotional benefits—as well as the respect—that come with legal marriage. And to care for their loved ones, gay people also need the legal rights that straight people get when they marry. There are over a thousand legal rights, protections, and responsibilities that are automatically granted to married couples, many of them granted by the federal government. Gay and lesbian couples simply want those same rights.

For example, when a man and a woman get married, they are automatically given the legal right to make medical decisions for each other in an emergency. They are automatically allowed to visit each other in a hospital intensive care unit. If one partner dies, the other automatically inherits the other's property and pension. If they choose to adopt a baby together, both automatically become the child's parents. And that's just a very short list of the kinds of legal rights and privileges that come with a marriage license.

✳ Can gay people get married?

In the United States (at the time I'm writing this answer), Massachusetts is the only state where gay people have the same exact legal right to marry as straight people. Gay people who live in any other state cannot get married under the same laws as straight people—and because of residency requirements in Massachusetts, gay people who live in other states can't go to Massachusetts to get married. (As spelled out in the U.S. Constitution, each state has the right to make its own laws concerning marriage.)

This answer is about to get more complicated and you're welcome to skip to the next question, but I guarantee that you'll be the most informed person among your friends about this issue if you take the time to read the whole answer.

A few other states have laws that allow gay people to enter into legally recognized committed relationships called "civil unions" or "domestic partnerships." These legally sanctioned relationships more or less come close to legal marriage, but the people who wrote the laws chose to call these marriages something other than "marriage" because they believe that "marriage" is only for a man and a woman, not for two people of the same sex. (Are you still with me?)

Because of the cynically named Defense of Marriage Act—which was signed into law in the middle of the night by then-President Bill Clinton—the federal government does not recognize marriages between people of the same sex. As you know from a previous answer, this is a big deal because there are very important rights granted by the federal government to heterosexual married couples, particularly those regarding Social Security, government pensions, and inheritance laws (including inheritance taxes, which is the tax you pay on money or property you inherit from someone, unless you're married to them). The federal government also refuses to honor civil unions or domestic partnerships.

The Defense of Marriage Act also allows states the right *not* to recognize marriages between people of the same sex performed in other states. (States are required by law to recognize heterosexual marriages performed in any other state). So, if your gay aunts from Massachusetts got married in Massachusetts and then moved to Ohio, the state of Ohio would consider their marriage to be invalid and, in any event, their legal Massachusetts marriage is not recognized by the federal government. (I don't think any of this is fair. And I don't understand why some people make such a big deal about two people who love each other and want to get married. Do you?)

To make up for the rights and privileges gay and lesbian

couples can't get through legal marriage, gay couples often draw up special legal documents. Unfortunately, the documents only cover some things and are not recognized in all states.

Suze, who is gay, told me that she never realized how important legal marriage was until her father was in a coma. "Life-and-death decisions were automatically in my mother's hands," she says, "without explanation or a legal struggle. She was his wife, and that was all that the doctors needed to know. As I watched my mother sign countless medical consent forms, I was struck by what the situation might look like if one day I was in that hospital bed and my female partner was the one trying to make the decisions. Even with legal documents drawn up for emergency situations, there is no guarantee that they would be honored."

Imagine for a minute what it would be like if your father was ill and the hospital wouldn't let your mom visit or wouldn't listen to her decisions about his medical treatment. Is there any question that this would be wrong and unfair? Unfortunately, this sort of thing can and does happen to gay and lesbian couples.

✳ Can gay people get married in other countries around the world?

In Canada, South Africa, Spain, the Netherlands, and Belgium, gay and lesbian couples can get married just like straight people. And in several other countries, including

Great Britain, they can get legal protections that come close to the legal protections given to married straight couples. (Did you notice that the world hasn't come to an end?) Unfortunately, when gay couples who are U.S. citizens get married in countries where it's allowed, their marriages are not considered legal by the U.S. government when they return home.

For more information about the ongoing marriage debate in the United States, have a look at the website for the Human Rights Campaign (www.hrc.org) or Freedom to Marry (www.freedomtomarry.org).

✱ My two moms had a commitment ceremony. Is that the same thing as getting married?

A "commitment ceremony" is a lot like a wedding: Two people invite their friends and family to witness an exchange of vows and to celebrate the couple's commitment to sharing their lives—but there is nothing legally binding about that commitment because it does not include a marriage license from the state. (Usually when straight couples have this kind of celebration, which is generally called a "wedding," they're also celebrating the fact that they're getting legally married: They've signed a state marriage license that's recognized by the federal government, by every state in the country, and around the world.)

For example, in June 1996, Barney and I had a commitment ceremony in the garden of a church across the street from our house in New York City. We had about two hundred guests, including our parents, my grandmother, our brothers and sisters, nieces and nephews, uncles and aunts, cousins, friends, neighbors, and colleagues. We had a friend conduct the ceremony (a sort of master of ceremonies), we exchanged vows and rings, and afterward we had a big party at our house to celebrate. To us, it was like a wedding, and in fact, whenever my grandmother talked about it, she called it a wedding. And while we feel just as committed to each other as two married people do, and love each other just as much as two married people do, we can't get a marriage license, so we're not protected by the laws that protect straight couples who get married.

Another example is Meg and Mal, from Cambridge, Massachusetts, but unlike my partner and me, they got legally married. They were among the first wave of couples to tie the knot at Boston's City Hall in 2004, soon after gay people were granted the legal right to marry in Massachusetts. Several months later they had a wedding, which was partly like a traditional wedding and partly a ceremony of their own invention. They walked down the aisle together, arm in arm. Meg wore a red velvet dress she'd had made especially for the occasion, and Mal wore a suit with a cummerbund that matched

Meg's dress. A friend performed the ceremony, and other friends and family members sang songs and read things they'd written especially for Meg and Mal.

At the reception afterward, everyone danced and Meg's grandfather made an emotional toast to his granddaughter and new granddaughter-in-law. For virtually all of their guests, it was the first time they had ever attended a legal wedding of a same-sex couple.

✳ Why are people against gay and lesbian couples getting married?

Some people think that marriage should only be for a man and a woman. Some believe this for religious reasons or because that's the way things have always been done. Others argue that allowing gay and lesbian couples to legally marry would somehow hurt straight family life and undermine heterosexual marriage. (I've never heard anyone explain exactly *how* allowing gay and lesbian couples to legally marry would damage heterosexual marriage and/or American family life—and they never explain it because they can't.)

Still others argue that if gay people are allowed to marry, then we're heading down a slippery slope that will lead to people wanting to marry their children, pets, or multiple partners (I'm not making this up). Because there are no organized groups lobbying for state-sanctioned marital status for such arrangements, I don't think we're likely to slip down any of those slopes any time soon. And if people wanted to enter into these unconventional relationships, I'm guessing that we can all agree that there are very good reasons why it would not be in anyone's best interest to extend legal status to them.

Some people think that the cost of insurance and other benefits will rise dramatically for business and government if gay people are given equal marriage rights because they will then be entitled to the same health insurance and other benefits granted to the partners of married hetero-sexuals. That has not been the case in states that have granted marriage rights or that permit civil unions. But even if that were the case, it's simply unfair to argue that it's okay to discriminate as long as it saves money.

Some people feel uncomfortable at the thought of their church holding weddings for gay couples. But it's impor-tant to remember that the religious part of a wedding ceremony and the legal part are separate things. The right to be married legally is a right granted by the government (by state governments, to be exact).

A lot of couples choose to add a religious component to their wedding and may choose to have their wedding conducted by a priest or rabbi (or other religious figure). This has nothing to do with legal marriage, and the gov-ernment plays no role in this aspect of marriage except to permit priests and rabbis to perform the legal part of a wedding ceremony.

No one who is in favor of granting gay people the legal right to marry argues that religious institutions should be forced to perform same-sex weddings. That decision is up to the various religious institutions themselves. Because of the separation of church and state, which is also spelled out in the U.S. Constitution, the government cannot force any religious group to perform marriages they don't want to. On the other hand, religious institutions should not be able to tell the government who can get a marriage license. (For more information on the subject of religion, please see Chapter 5, "God and Religion.")

✻ Are all people against gay people getting married?

No. A lot of Americans (a majority of younger people and less than a majority of older people) are in favor of allowing gay people to legally marry, and more than half of all Americans are in favor of granting gay people the same (or similar) rights of marriage as long as it's called something other than "marriage."

I believe gay and lesbian couples should have the right to legally marry, and I disagree with all the arguments made in opposition to legal marriage rights for gay couples. Religious beliefs, cultural traditions, and myths are no excuse for discrimination. Committed gay and lesbian couples should have all the same legal privileges and responsibilities enjoyed by straight couples, whether it's called a marriage, a domestic partnership, or a civil union. Anything less is unfair and discriminatory.

✳ Can gay people have children?

Yes, lesbian and gay people can have children. Many gay men and women, like many heterosexuals, want to be parents. But because two men, and because two women, can't have a baby by having sex, gay and lesbian couples who choose to have children do so through a variety of methods, including adoption (except in those states where gay couples are not allowed to adopt) and alternative insemination.

Also, gay people who came to terms with their sexual orientation later in life may have children from a previous heterosexual marriage. These gay parents often raise their kids on their own, jointly with their ex-spouses, and/or with their new same-sex partners.

✳ Will their children be gay too?

According to all the studies that have been done, children raised by parents who are gay are no more or less likely to be gay or lesbian than children raised by straight parents. Think about it: Most gay kids were raised by straight parents and that didn't make any of us straight.

chapter 4
sex

Sex is a topic that requires a lot more discussion than I can provide in this brief chapter. You'll find some basic information here, but if you're considering becoming sexually active—whether you're male or female, gay or straight—I very strongly recommend that you find out more information about sex in general, and about safer sex in particular, before you do anything. There are lots of books on this topic, a few of which you'll find listed in Chapter 9, "Resources." The one I like best and consider required reading for *every* young person is *Doing It Right: Making Smart, Safe, and Satisfying Choices About Sex*, by Bronwen Pardes.

✳ What exactly do you mean by "sex"?

When I was in college, this was a subject my friends and I usually couldn't agree on. Some people thought that anything you did where you and your partner got sexually excited was sex. Others thought that only vaginal inter- course (where a man's penis enters a woman's vagina) was sex and that everything else was just fooling around. And still others didn't consider it sex unless you both had an orgasm (an intense feeling of satisfaction and release that you can experience on your own through masturbation or when having sex with another person). I didn't think any of these definitions worked all that well, especially the penis-in-vagina definition for sex, because that left out gay and lesbian couples entirely.

Eventually, I came up with my own definition of what it means to have sex, one that includes all sorts of things that people might do together to give each other sexual pleasure. These include kissing, caressing, cuddling, mutual masturbation (using hands to stimu- late each other's genitals), oral sex (using the mouth to stimulate the other person's genitals), vaginal sex (where a penis goes into a vagina), and anal intercourse (where a man's penis enters his male or female part- ner's anus). Some people feel that it's not sex unless someone has an orgasm, but lots of people have sex without having orgasms.

✳ Why would two men want to have sex with each other? Why would two women want to have sex with each other?

When two people feel attracted to each other and/or they fall in love, it's perfectly normal for them to want to be physically close, to kiss and touch each other, and to get sexually excited. The urge to have sex is a basic part of the human experience, and it's a very powerful urge. Just as a man and woman can experience these pleasurable feelings, two women or two men can also share these very strong emotional and sexual feelings for each other.

Sometimes a man and woman have sex because they want to have a child. Because sex between two men or between two women can't lead to pregnancy, this isn't a reason for gay or lesbian couples to have sex.

✳ How do gay and lesbian people have sex? What do they do?

This is often the question that many young people (and adults, too!) are most curious to have answered. One twelve-year-old girl recently e-mailed me asking if gay people *try* to have sex. I thought for a moment about what she was asking and realized that given what she knew from her fourth-grade sexual reproduction class, sex between two men or between two women just didn't seem to make sense. Without a penis and a vagina, she wondered, how

87

could gay and lesbian couples have sex? Well, if you think of sex only as penis-in-vagina sexual intercourse, then gay and lesbian couples don't have sex. However, this is not the only way to define sex.

There are many things that gay and lesbian couples do to give each other sexual pleasure. Depending on what the couple likes to do and what makes them feel good, they may choose to: kiss and cuddle, caress each other's body, touch each other's genitals, and engage in oral or anal sex. Female couples may use a dildo—an object that's shaped like a penis—to penetrate each other, or they may touch each other's genitals with their hands and mouths.

Of course, there are important responsibilities for people to consider even before they begin a sexual relationship. Caring and responsible people take steps to reduce the risk of getting or passing along HIV (the virus that causes AIDS) or another sexually transmitted disease (more on that later in this chapter). And if the couple includes a man and a woman, it's extremely important to know about birth control and to do what's necessary to avoid an unplanned pregnancy.

✳ Do gay people have sex more often than straight people?

From everything I've read, the average gay man or gay woman has sex about as often as the average straight man or straight woman.

However, you will hear some activists who fight against equal rights for gay people claim that all gay men have hundreds, even thousands, of sexual partners every year. In spreading this myth, these anti-gay activists hope to turn public opinion against gay people and hurt efforts to extend equal rights to gay men and lesbians. The fact is, there are some gay men who have many sexual partners over the course of a weekend, a year, or a lifetime. And the same is true of some straight men as well (and some lesbians and straight women too), but no one would ever argue that straight people don't deserve equal rights because some straight people have many sexual partners.

✳ Do you have to have sex to know if you're gay or lesbian?

No, you don't. And you don't need to have sex to know if you're straight, either. For the complete answer to this question, please see Chapter 1, "The Basic Stuff."

✳ If you have sex with someone of the same sex just one time, does that make you gay or lesbian? If you have sex with someone of the opposite sex just one time, does that make you straight?

When I was a teenager, after I had my first sexual experience with a man and realized for sure I was gay, I decided that

I didn't want to be gay. So I figured if I had sex with a woman, the experience would somehow make me straight. It didn't work. What I discovered, instead, was that trying to have sex with women made me very upset because it wasn't something I really wanted to do; I didn't have feelings of sexual attraction for them, so having sex with a woman felt unnatural to me.

What I didn't understand at that age was that no sexual experience with a man or a woman, whether it's a passionate kiss, mutual masturbation, or intercourse, has any impact on whether you're gay, straight, or bisexual. The experience can even be pleasurable, but it makes no difference. Your sexual orientation can't be changed by one sexual experience, one hundred sexual experiences, or by prayer, therapy, or anything else.

You may be surprised to learn that some straight people have had homosexual experiences and that some gay men and women have had heterosexual experiences. Some people have even learned that they enjoy having sex with both men and women. But while a sexual experience may help you *recognize* what you really feel deep down, as it did for me, no sexual experience has ever changed anyone's true sexual orientation. Your feelings of sexual attraction are yours to keep and enjoy for the rest of your life, but you can't do anything to change them.

✳ I like being physical (not in a sexual way) with my buddies. I like being affectionate with my girlfriends. Does that mean I'm gay?

That means you're like everybody else, no matter what their sexual orientation. Most human beings like being physical with their friends and with people they care about. It's human nature. That's why people hug, walk arm in arm, hold hands, pat each other on the back, and so forth. (In some places, like India and Morocco, it's common to see straight guys walking hand in hand or arm in arm.) Being physically affectionate with people you care about is one of the joys of life. Unfortunately, because so many people are afraid of being thought of as gay, they're more likely today to hold back and not do what comes naturally.

✳ Do gay men find women physically disgusting? Do lesbians find men physically disgusting?

Over the years, it's been rare for me to hear from gay men or from lesbians that they find people of the opposite sex physically disgusting. It's more a matter of just not being interested sexually.

✳ If I'm not gay, do I need to worry about HIV/AIDS?

Absolutely. Everybody needs to know about the full range of diseases that can be passed from one person to another during sex, including HIV, which is the most dangerous of sexually transmitted diseases (STDs). And it's important to know about these diseases and how to protect yourself *before* you become sexually active.

STDs don't care what your feelings of sexual attraction are. They're just looking for a way to get from one person to another. In the case of AIDS, a potentially deadly disease of the immune system, HIV (the virus that causes AIDS) can be passed from one partner to another during oral, vaginal, or anal sex. And don't think you can tell just from looking at someone whether he or she has HIV or any other STD. That's a dangerous myth. A man or woman can look and feel perfectly healthy and still be infected with any number of STDs, including HIV.

✳ Are gay men more likely to get HIV than other people?

When the AIDS virus first appeared in the United States, gay men were among the first to be infected. During the early years of the epidemic, in the 1980s, most of the people who were infected and later died were gay men (this was before there were effective anti-viral treatments to help control the progression of the disease). But around the world and more and more in the United States, AIDS is a disease that affects both men and women, regardless of their sexual orientation. In fact, worldwide, the majority of people who are infected with the AIDS virus are straight. The rate at which women are getting HIV is increasing, and young people make up the fastest-growing population of new HIV infections.

✳ What can people do to keep from getting HIV and other sexually transmitted diseases?

The many different kinds of sexually transmitted diseases (HIV, syphilis, gonorrhea, and herpes, among others) can be passed from one partner to the other through oral, anal, and vaginal sex. But if you take the proper precautions, you can avoid getting one, so it's important to educate yourself *before* you begin engaging in any kind of sexual activity with another person.

There is only one way to completely avoid sexually transmitted diseases, and that is by not having oral, anal, or vaginal sex. It is possible to have a sexual relationship with someone without engaging in these behaviors. It's very pleasurable—and very safe—to kiss, cuddle, caress, and touch your partner's genitals with your hands.

People who choose to have oral, anal, and vaginal sex can avoid STDs by using protection, such as condoms or dental dams. (Condoms are devices made out of latex that can be worn over the penis during oral sex and intercourse. Dental dams are squares of latex that can be placed over the vagina when performing oral sex on a woman.) These methods are effective in preventing most sexually trans-mitted diseases, and condoms are great for preventing unplanned pregnancies—but only if they are used correctly and are used every time a person has sex.

There is so much more to learn about this subject than what I'm able to cover here, so please educate yourself. Talk to your parents, talk to educators and counselors, read *Doing It Right*, and consult the resources in Chapter 9.

chapter 5
god and religion

When it comes to homosexuality, religion is a subject that generates more heat and less light than any other. For example, people of many different faiths feel strongly that being gay goes against the teachings of their particular religion, yet they're generally not open to discussing an opposing point of view. This can be very painful for gay people, especially those who have strong religious faith. So, not surprisingly, I often hear from gay people who have trouble figuring out how to cope with the conflict between their sexual orientation and their religion. And I hear from straight religious people who face the challenge of reconciling their beliefs with their love for someone who is gay.

Perhaps the information in this chapter will help people who are on both sides of the divide gain a better understanding of a topic that will likely be debated and discussed for many years to come.

✳ At church, my minister says that homosexuality is a sin. Is that true?

Many religions and many religious people believe that homosexuality is a sin, but people have all kinds of views on this subject. There are religious leaders of all faiths who don't think homosexuality is a sin, who don't think that having a gay or lesbian relationship is a sin or that it's immoral.

Some religions teach that it's a sin to be gay. Your religion may also say that masturbation, premarital sex, and birth control are all sinful as well. Do you agree? Some people will choose to ignore what their religion says about something if it's something they want to do, but will stand by their religion when it condemns something that makes them uncomfortable, like homosexuality. Ultimately, while religion can provide a guide to how we lead our lives, we each have to decide what is right and wrong for ourselves.

I like what retired Episcopal Bishop John Shelby Spong has to say on this subject. When asked by PFLAG (Parents, Families and Friends of Lesbians and Gays) whether, in his opinion, God regards homosexuality as sinful, he answered:

> Contemporary research is uncovering new facts that are producing rising conviction that homosexuality, far from being a sickness, sin, perversion, or unnatural act, is a healthy, natural, and affirming form of human sexuality for some people. . . . Our prejudice rejects people or things outside our understanding. But the God of creation speaks and declares, "I have looked out on everything I have made and 'behold it [is] very good'" (Genesis 1:31). The word of God in Christ says that we are loved, valued, redeemed, and counted as precious no matter how we might be valued by a prejudiced world.

✳ Does God love gay people?

Not everyone believes in God. But, if there is a God, I like to think that God is a loving God, and that a loving God would love all of his/her creations.

✳ What do the different religions have to say about gay people?

Here is a very brief survey of the official views of the major religions in the United States on the subject of homosexuality. Keep in mind that, despite official stated positions, there is often strong disagreement among the different denominations, different religious leaders, different congregations, and individual members of a congregation when it comes to opinions about homosexuality.

The Episcopal Church lets openly gay people join the denomination and does not consider homosexuality a sin. They ordained the first openly gay bishop in the United States in 2003, which was a source of much controversy.

The Lutherans welcome openly gay people, and allow gay and lesbian people to serve as members of the clergy if they remain celibate. Presbyterians welcome openly gay and lesbian people, although openly gay, sexually active people cannot serve as Presbyterian ministers.

The Roman Catholic Church permits openly gay people to join, but considers homosexuality morally wrong and a sin if practiced. The Baptists officially let openly gay people join, although homosexuality is considered to be a sin, but the American Baptists and the Southern Baptists differ on their views, and individual churches set their own rules.

The United Methodists let openly gay people join and do not officially consider homosexuality a sin. Mormons (The Church of Jesus Christ of Latter-day Saints) do not let openly gay people join, considers homosexuality a sin, and recommends chastity for homosexuals.

Muslims do not let openly gay people join, consider homosexuality one of the worst sins, and encourage homosexuals to change. Orthodox Jews also believe that homosexuality is an abomination, but the Conservative and Reform movements of Judaism welcome gay and lesbian people to their congregations, and in 2006, Conservative Jews joined Reform Jews in deciding to ordain gay rabbis and in allowing rabbis to perform same-sex commitment ceremonies and weddings.

Buddhists openly welcome gay people, ordain them, and don't consider homosexuality a sin. The Unitarian Universalist Association of Congregations welcomes gay men and women in all church roles. And the Universal Fellowship of the Metropolitan Community Churches (UFMCC) was founded specifically to welcome gay, lesbian, bisexual, and transgender people.

✳ Doesn't the Bible teach that homosexuality is wrong?

The Bible does not discuss sexual orientation as we understand it today, although it does on occasion address sexual behavior. For example, the Bible's "Holiness Code" (the Book of Leviticus) bans sexual acts between men (the Bible says nothing about sex between women). But as Peter J. Gomes, an American Baptist minister and professor of Christian morals at Harvard University noted in a *New York Times* editorial, "[The code] also prohibits eating raw meat, planting two different kinds of seed in the same field, and wearing garments with two different kinds of yarn. Tattoos, adultery, and sexual intercourse during a woman's menstrual period are similarly outlawed."

While many people continue to draw inspiration from the Bible, most have rejected many of the outdated laws and customs first set down in the Bible centuries ago. And just as Christians have rejected the Bible's teachings as justification for slavery, I think that all Christians will eventually reject the Bible's teachings on homosexuality as an excuse to condemn gay and lesbian people and deny them equal rights.

✳ Haven't religious leaders also said good things about gay people?

Yes, and over the years, many religious leaders have challenged the official anti-gay rules and teachings of their respective religions. Some religious leaders have worked quietly within their denominations to change anti-gay rules, and others have made very public statements and protests. Some religious leaders have also taken active roles in the gay civil rights effort since it first began in the 1950s.

In more recent times, several ministers went to New Paltz, New York, in 2004, to demonstrate in favor of same-sex marriage. They did so by performing marriage ceremonies for twenty-five gay and lesbian couples. The marriages were ultimately not recognized by the state of

New York, but the ministers made a very powerful statement of support for gay civil rights and same-sex marriage.

✳ What did Jesus have to say about homosexuality?

Nothing. Despite the many things that some Christian religious leaders have said against gay and lesbian people, not one of them was ever alleged to have been said by Jesus Christ.

✳ Can gay people become straight through prayer?

No. Gay people cannot become straight through prayer. That idea is just as unrealistic as thinking that heterosexual people can become gay through prayer. Still, many parents have encouraged their gay and lesbian children to pray for a "healing." That is exactly what Mary Griffith, who once held Christian fundamentalist beliefs, encouraged her teenage gay son, Bobby, to do. Mary said that at the time, "We hoped God would heal him of being gay. According to God's word, as we were led to understand it, Bobby had to repent or God would damn him to hell and eternal punishment. Blindly, I accepted the idea that it is God's nature to torment and intimidate us."

So Bobby prayed, all the while fearing he would be punished by God for his homosexuality. He wrote in his diary,

"Why did you do this to me, God? Am I going to hell? That's the question that's always drilling little holes in the back of my mind. Please don't send me to hell. I'm really not that bad, am I? I want to be good. I want to amount to something. I need your seal of approval. If I had that, I would be happy. Life is so cruel and unfair."

A year and a half after this diary entry, still tormented by guilt and despondent over his unanswered prayers, Bobby committed suicide.

In a letter to gay young people printed in a San Francisco newspaper, Bobby's mother later wrote,

I firmly believe—though I did not, back then—that my son Bobby's suicide is the end result of homophobia and ignorance within most Protestant and Catholic churches, and consequently within society, our public schools, our own family.

Bobby was not drunk, nor did he use drugs. It's just that we could never accept him for who he was—a gay person. . . . Looking back, I realize how depraved it was to instill false guilt in an innocent child's conscience, causing a distorted image of life, God, and self, leaving little if any feeling of personal worth. Had I viewed my son's life with a pure heart, I would have recognized him as a tender spirit in God's eyes.

The story of Mary Griffith and her son is told in a book called *Prayers for Bobby*.

✳ Are there churches just for gay people?

Yes. The Universal Fellowship of the Metropolitan Community Churches, whose membership is primarily gay and lesbian, has a few hundred congregations in the United States and around the world.

✳ Are there other places of worship specifically for gay and lesbian people who are religious?

Yes. For example, most major cities have a gay and lesbian synagogue (for Jewish people). And there are organizations all across the country specifically for gay and lesbian people who are Catholic, Jewish, Episcopal, Lutheran, Muslim, Mormon, and just about any other religious denomination you can name (see Chapter 9, "Resources").

✳ If I'm lesbian or gay and my religious beliefs tell me that what I am is wrong, what can I do?

Many people, young and old, have written to me over the years about conflicts between their religious beliefs and their sexual feelings. Often, what they know in their hearts about themselves has clashed harshly with the teachings of their religion. This is a personal challenge for which there is no single answer.

For Mark, who thought he was going to hell because of what his pastor said in church, the personal conflict was enormous. Finally, he came to terms with his sexuality and what his church had taught him. "I was having anxiety attacks every day. There were six to nine months of hell. I couldn't breathe. I remember sitting in church every Sunday feeling very nervous. Then something just snapped in my brain. It was the thought of going to college and planning out my adult life. It was the promise of love. I started imagining this guy I would fall in love with. It was the power of love out there that overpowered the bad feelings. And then I read everything I could about gay people and learned about gay religious groups and that there were people who read the Bible who were gay and were also religious. That did it for me."

Carolyn Mobley also struggled with her sexuality, which she once believed was sinful. But then as a college student she realized that her sexuality was not sinful but, instead, a gift from God. I met Carolyn several years ago, when she was an assistant pastor at a Metropolitan Community Church. I hope that her thoughts on this subject, which follow, will help you think in new ways about what you have been taught and what you know to be true about yourself or about a gay person you know.

Carolyn gives credit to the Reverend Martin Luther King, Jr., with helping her come to terms with being a lesbian. She told me, "Dr. King's commitment to disobeying unjust laws had a profound impact on my thinking. I began to question the things that I was told to do. Are they really right? Are they right if I'm told they're right by a person in a position of authority? I began to realize that parents could steer you wrong. Preachers, God knows, could steer you wrong. They were all fallible human beings; they could make mistakes. That really changed my way of looking at myself and the world. And it certainly helped me reevaluate the message I was getting from the church about homosexuality. It made me examine more closely what the Scripture had to say about it."

After examining the Scripture, Carolyn came to the following conclusion: "God didn't deliver me from my sexuality. God delivered me from guilt and shame and gave me a sense of pride and wholeness that I really needed. My sexuality was a gift from God, and so is everyone's sexuality, no matter how it's oriented. It's a gift to be able to love." I couldn't agree more.

chapter 6
school

Education and what you're likely to learn at school about homosexuality and gay people is the focus of this chapter. Unfortunately, very little, if anything, is taught at most grammar, middle, and high schools about gay and lesbian people, gay history, or gay issues. But there are exceptions. Some schools have clubs, often called Gay-Straight Alliances (GSAs), where gay topics are discussed. Some schools invite special guests to speak about gay and lesbian issues. Some have shown educational documentaries (for a list of the available documentaries, have a look at the website for the Gay, Lesbian and Straight Education Network, www.glsen.org). Others have public bulletin boards where news stories about gay issues are posted. Some school libraries have books about the subject. And some individual teachers have included gay and lesbian issues in their regular lessons, usually in the context of English, health, or social studies classes.

✱ Can you give an example of a teacher who includes gay issues in his lessons?

Chris Lord was teaching sixth-grade American history and seventh-grade civics at a private school in Maryland when I first met him. He included gay and lesbian issues when he thought it was appropriate. He said, "We did a civil rights movement unit and it was most appropriate to use something current, like the gay rights movement." Chris said that more often than not, the subject came up as a natural part of class discussions. "For example, in my sixth-grade class, I questioned someone's use of the word 'redneck.' Then we went through a lot of the put-down words people use, and the kids locked on to the word 'faggot.' That led to a thirty-five-minute discussion."

One reason Chris thinks students were comfortable discussing gay issues in his class was that he usually volunteered the fact he has a gay father. Chris told me: "On the wall next to my desk, I had a picture of my dad and his partner." Chris also maintained a bulletin board in his class where news items were posted about gay issues.

✳ How do kids react to the subject when it comes up in class?

Depending on the school, the class, the age of the students, and the attitude of the teacher, students' reactions will vary. They may be curious and eager to talk, quietly respectful, embarrassed, confused, or even hostile.

When Erica spoke up in her civics class during a discussion about gay civil rights, her twelve-year-old classmates listened quietly and respectfully. It wasn't easy for her to overcome her fear, but she did it. Knowing that her teacher, Chris Lord, had a gay father helped give her the confidence to say what was on her mind. Erica told me: "I said I thought it was wrong what most kids think and they should learn more about it before they have an opinion. Most kids think being gay is sick and nasty and that gay people have a choice. I just said there's nothing wrong with being gay, that my uncle is gay and he's perfectly fine. My classmates agreed with me that it wasn't wrong."

Jake can't imagine speaking up in class at his small high school outside Portland, Oregon, especially after a recent incident where a student defended gay people during a class debate. He recalled, "The kids started yelling at him that he was a faggot, and he sort of backed down and said that it wasn't that he liked gay people or anything, but that there wasn't anything wrong with them. There were kids just screaming at him, saying things like 'God created Adam and Eve, not Adam and Steve.' It was kind of getting extreme and I was wondering if the teacher would stop them but he just sat there and didn't say anything." Jake didn't say anything either, because he doesn't want anyone to know he's gay and was afraid of drawing attention to himself.

Mae knew she would be drawing attention to herself when she gave a persuasive speech in her twelfth-grade English class on the subject of gay people. After ninth grade, when her ex-girlfriend spread rumors about her being gay, Mae started at a new high school and, within a few months after arriving, she began telling people that she was gay. By twelfth grade, everybody knew.

When it came time to decide on a topic for her persuasive speech, Mae knew she wanted to do something different from her classmates' speeches. "Most people were doing it on abortion or about lowering the drinking age. I wanted to tell everybody what it was like to be gay and why same-sex marriage should be legalized." Still, she was nervous. "Up to this time, nobody had ever said anything to my face that was negative, but I was afraid of the snickering and the whispering. I didn't know how people would react.

"I started by asking how they would like to live in a world where you couldn't marry the man or woman you loved, you couldn't tell your parents about a crush. Then I said that that's how it was for me, for gay people. Everybody was paying attention and it was all eyes on me, including my teacher. She'd been looking down at her papers. Then when I said the word 'gay,' she looked up at me and looked at me dead on. I don't think she expected something quite that different. When I finished, it was kind of silent at first. Most people were shocked that I had the nerve to talk about this. After class, a lot of them told me what a good job I'd done."

✳ How do parents react to their children being taught about gay and lesbian issues?

Some parents are pleased that the subject is being taught, because they themselves are gay, or because they have lesbian or gay family or friends, or because they think that teaching appreciation for differences among people is a good thing for schools to do. Others have no particular opinion about it. Some think it's inappropriate or wrong. And still others think that anything positive said by a teacher about gay people is grounds for being fired.

✳ Why do some parents object to teaching students about gay people?

Some parents object to students being taught about sexuality in general, or they may believe that sex education should be taught at home or in religious institutions. Other parents believe that by talking about homosexuality, you will encourage students to become gay. Of course, you can't make anyone gay. But by teaching students the truth instead of the old negative myths, you can make them better informed, more understanding, and more comfortable with their own sexuality and the sexuality of other people.

Another reason some parents object to teaching children about this subject is that they have strong, negative beliefs about homosexuality and gay people. They want to pass these beliefs on to their children and don't want them to hear any other points of view on this subject, especially at school.

✳ Are there gay and lesbian teachers?

There have always been gay and lesbian teachers, but until recent years, nearly all teachers kept their sexual orientation a secret. This has begun to change, especially at colleges and universities and some high schools. And there are now organizations for gay and lesbian teachers in major cities across the country. But when it comes to middle schools and grade schools, it's more unusual to find any teachers who are openly gay, although that's starting to change too.

✳ Why do they keep it a secret?

Gay and lesbian teachers have kept their sexual orientation secret for a number of reasons. Most important, they've feared losing their jobs and/or they've been afraid of negative reactions from their colleagues, administrators, or from parents who object to gay people being teachers. And because relatively few teachers are openly gay, those who are open often find themselves in the position of being pioneers. Charting new territory is never easy, especially when your job may be on the line.

Not many years ago, lesbian and gay teachers whose secret was found out were fired from their jobs and lost their teaching licenses. There are now laws in many places that protect gay and lesbian people from being fired simply because they are gay, but that depends on local or state laws or the policy of the school. And even where there are laws protecting gay people from being fired, teachers may still be afraid that their careers could be harmed if it became known that they were gay, especially if they work with young children.

✳ Why would anyone object to gay and lesbian people being teachers?

Some people mistakenly believe that gay and lesbian teachers will influence their students to become gay (which we know is not possible). Others believe that gay people are sinful and immoral, so they think gay teachers are poor role models for children. Still others mistakenly believe that gay men and lesbians are more likely to be child molesters. Not only is this untrue, studies have shown that gay people are *less* likely than straight people to molest children. (Heterosexual males are the most likely people to molest children.)

✳ If I'm being teased or called names because I'm gay or because someone thinks I'm gay, is there anyone at school I can talk to?

With any luck, there is a school nurse, counselor, teacher, or administrator whom you can talk to. At some schools there are administrators, counselors, and/or teachers who put a "Safe Zone" sticker outside their office or classroom so that gay and lesbian students or those who have questions about gay issues will know they are welcome.

If there is no one at your school you think you can talk to and you can't talk to your parents, contact one of the resources listed in Chapter 9.

✳ Are there any school organizations for young people who are gay or who think they're gay, or for straight people who have friends or family members who are gay?

Yes. There are thousands of Gay-Straight Alliances (GSAs) and similar groups at high schools (and a growing number of middle schools) across the country for gay, lesbian, bisexual, and transgender teenagers and their friends and supporters. Some of the groups have been started by gay and lesbian young people, some have been started by straight students who have gay and lesbian friends or family members, and some have been started by teachers and administrators.

One of the first high school GSAs was started in 1989, at Concord Academy, a private high school in Concord, Massachusetts. A ninth grader whose mother was gay was upset by all the anti-gay comments she heard around school. So with the hope of changing things at Concord Academy, the student spoke to her history teacher, Kevin Jennings—who happened to be gay—about starting a student group of some kind. They wanted everyone to feel welcome, so together they came up with the name "Gay-Straight Alliance." (Kevin later founded the Gay, Lesbian and Straight Education Network—GLSEN—which helps support students and teachers who form and lead GSAs. See www.glsen.org.)

In general, the goal of the GSAs is to provide a supportive and safe place for open discussion between gay and non-gay students about the issues gay people face in school, with their families, and in their communities. They also often try to educate the larger school community by organizing events like the Day of Silence, which is a day each school year when students stay silent for part or

114

all of the school day to symbolize how gay people get silenced in schools and society every day. Other events include Ally Week, a week in which GSA members ask other students to be allies against prejudice. And GSA members also advocate for new local and state laws protecting the rights of gay students.

GSAs are open to all students, and no student has to identify his or her own sexual orientation. If there isn't a GSA at your school, consider starting one. You can contact www.glsen.org for more information.

✳ Are things different for gay people once they get to college?

In most cases, yes, although it depends on the college or university you attend. Some schools are very welcoming and you'll find lots of out gay people. Other schools are either not so welcoming or are even hostile (like schools that are run by religious institutions that have an anti-gay doctrine).

So when you're researching which schools to apply to, if you want to go to a school where everyone is welcome, you can usually figure out the kind of school it is by looking at the list of student organizations and the course offerings. For example, there are lots of colleges and universities that have gay and lesbian studies programs, and there are a lot more schools that offer at least a few courses on the subject. You can start your research by looking at a school's website and reviewing its student organizations and course offerings. (GLSEN offers a simple brochure you can use to help figure out what to look for and good questions to ask.)

Jazmin wasn't so sure how welcome she would be at the community college she was planning to attend in Queens, New York, if anyone knew she was gay. And once she started going to classes, she quickly discovered that a lot of her classmates had negative opinions of gay people. Jazmin is shy and doesn't usually say a lot in any of her classes, but when the subject of homosexuality came up in her human sexuality class and her fellow students were saying things like "it's a choice" and "it's a sin," she knew she had to do something. "Somehow," she said, "I raised my hand. I wanted them to understand a little bit."

After talking about her own experience of being a lesbian, the same classmates who had had so many negative things to say about gay people thanked her for coming out. "One guy said to me, 'You have a lot of guts to come out after hearing everyone say what they did. Thank you. I didn't think about these things before.' I was scared to say what I did, before and even after I did it. But I don't regret it. And it doesn't matter if my classmates don't accept me or my sexual orientation, as long as what I say makes them wonder just a bit about why they believe it's wrong."

✳ Were things different for *you* once you got to college?

Well, not as different as you might think. The college I went to, Vassar College, was very different from my high school and, for the times, very accepting of gay and lesbian students. There had been a gay student group on campus since 1970.

But the problem for me wasn't the school. *I* was the problem. I left home a very conflicted seventeen-year-old gay guy who didn't want to be gay and arrived at college a seventeen-year-old gay guy who didn't want to be gay. So while there were plenty of gay people for me to meet at school, I was terrified that anyone would think I was gay. And I was still hoping that my feelings of same-sex attraction would somehow go away. At the same time, I found it exciting to be around other gay people and I really wanted to have a boyfriend. I was a mess.

If I could have given my seventeen-year-old self the advice I find so easy to give now, I would have said: "All colleges have counseling programs, so make an appointment at the student health center and talk to someone who has experience dealing with issues concerning sexuality. Talking to a professional about your feelings will help you deal with your conflicts and help you learn to accept yourself for who you are."

Of course that wasn't what I did—only people who had

real problems needed to talk to a counselor, and I didn't want to think that I was the kind of person who needed professional help. So instead, I spent a lot of time and energy sorting out my feelings on my own, eventually confiding in a couple of close friends, who were of some help. But it took me a lot longer to figure things out than it would have if I'd sought professional help. By not doing so, I made things way more difficult for myself than they needed to be. Maybe that's why I'm now so quick to recommend to many of the people who write to me that they talk to a professional counselor. There's no need to suffer the way I did when there is help out there, whether you're in middle school, high school, or just heading off to college.

chapter 7
parades, activism, and discrimination

I f you walk around the neighborhood in New York City where my partner and I live, you'll see rainbow flags displayed from buildings and rainbow decals in residential and shop windows. These are symbols of gay pride; they show that the people displaying them are comfortable being open about their sexual orientation, and that my neighborhood welcomes gay people.

Of course, this hasn't always been the case—until more recent years, the average gay person was much more likely to hide his sexual orientation than to proudly display a symbol of it in his window or on a car bumper. So when gay people participate in gay pride parades and festivals, they're in part celebrating the strides the gay civil rights movement has made. However, as you'll see from the topics covered in this chapter, there is quite a ways to go before gay people are treated just like everyone else, which is why a lot of people—both gay and straight—are active in the ongoing gay civil rights movement.

✳ Why do gay people have special parades?

Every June (and sometimes May or July or another month), gay and lesbian people hold parades and festivals across the United States and in countries around the world. Almost all of these celebrations mark the anniversary of the Stonewall riots, an important event in the gay civil rights movement.

In the early-morning hours of June 28, 1969, the New York City police raided the Stonewall Inn, a gay bar in Greenwich Village. In those days it was routine for the police to harass, arrest, and sometimes beat up gay and lesbian patrons at gay bars and clubs. Most often, the bar patrons did their best to avoid trouble and keep from being arrested, because you could lose your job if anyone found out you were gay. But this time, the gay men and lesbians at the bar fought back, and that led to a riot that lasted for a couple of days. Publicity from this event led to the formation of new (and more assertive) gay and lesbian civil rights organizations across the country, especially at colleges and universities.

✳ Why do people go to gay pride parades and festivals?

People go to these events for many different reasons. Some go to demand equal rights for gay people. Some gay people go to have a good time or to show their sense of pride in being themselves. Other gay and lesbian people go so they can be around a lot of other gay people. And some straight people go to show their support for their family and friends who are gay and for gay people in general.

Emily went to her first gay pride parade in New York City when she was in college, just after she came out to her friends and family. "Arriving at the gay pride parade and being surrounded by all these people who were just like me floored me!" she said. "All of a sudden I was part of something bigger than me, among people who understood exactly what I had gone through because they had gone through it themselves. I felt so proud to be there—proud of myself for having had the courage to come out, proud of the gay community for being so loud and proud about who we are, and proud that this parade celebrated my diversity. After years of struggling with being so different from most people around me, suddenly I belonged."

I remember the first time I went to a gay pride parade in New York City. I was in my early twenties and it was amazing to see so many gay and lesbian people in one place. And such variety! It made me feel good about myself to know that I wasn't alone and to see so many gay people who looked happy. And for once it was nice to be in the majority!

✳ When did the gay civil rights movement start?

In Germany, gay rights organizations were first started in the late 1800s, but were later wiped out by the Nazis. In 1924, Henry Gerber attempted to start the first gay organization in the United States, but the U.S. gay rights movement didn't really get going until the 1950s. That's when a handful of men and women very courageously, and successfully, formed a number of different organizations specifically for gay people (most often they called themselves "homosexuals" or "homophiles" back then). Attitudes toward gay people were very negative in those days, and people were afraid to even go to meetings or use their real names.

At meetings of these groups, like the Mattachine Society and the Daughters of Bilitis, people talked about the problems they faced. Some organizations fought for the right of gay and lesbian people to get together at bars without being harassed or arrested by the police. And they also published the first magazines for gay women and men. However, it wasn't until the late 1960s, following the

Stonewall riots in New York City, that the gay civil rights effort became a national movement to be reckoned with.

✳ I've heard that gay people want special rights. No one should have special rights. Don't you agree?

I agree that no one should have special rights. But what gay and lesbian people want is *equal* rights. They want to work just like everyone else, without having to worry that they're going to get fired because they're gay. They want to go to school like everyone else, without being called names or getting physically attacked because they're gay. They want the right to get married just like everyone else (see Chapter 3, "Dating, Marriage, and Kids" for more information on this). They want to be treated equally.

The people who claim that gay men and women want "special rights" are trying to make you believe that gay men and women want something more than what everyone else has. That's how they get people to vote against laws that protect gay people from discrimination.

I think we can agree that no one deserves special rights. But we can also agree that all people deserve equal rights.

✳ Aren't gay people already protected by laws that forbid discrimination?

Yes and no. In the United States there are many states and

cities that have laws that protect gay and lesbian people from discrimination. There are companies and colleges and universities that protect gay people from discrimination. And federal employees who are gay are protected by law. But laws forbidding discrimination against gay people are more of a patchwork quilt of mostly state and local laws than blanket protection. There is no national law that protects gay people from discrimination in the same way that all other Americans are already protected because of their race, religion, age, disability, etc. That's why you hear in the news about people fighting for local, state, and national laws to protect gay people from discrimination.

✱ How are gay people discriminated against today?

Things are much better today than when the early gay rights organizations were founded in the 1950s. In those days gay people didn't even *think* about being open about their sexual orientation, because anyone who was found out would likely have been fired from his or her job, been thrown out of college, forced to move out of their apartment, or even committed to a hospital for the mentally ill. And there was nowhere for you to turn when these things happened. There were no gay legal organizations, no anti-discrimination laws, no pro-gay politicians, nothing.

The world has changed a lot for gay people since the

1950s, but problems of discrimination remain; people are still fired because they're gay, and there are many places in the United States where this is legal. Gay and lesbian couples, no matter how many years they've been together, are denied the federal protections given to heterosexual married couples, and only a few states give these couples the right to legalize their relationships through civil unions or marriage. And openly gay people are forbidden to serve in the military.

And that's not all. Gay and lesbian parents are still sometimes denied custody of their children in divorce cases, simply because they're gay. Gay boys are not allowed to join the Boy Scouts (how ridiculous is that?). Gay teens are routinely harassed at schools across the country. Some Gay-Straight Alliances have even been forced to go to court to win the right to meet on school grounds. And gay people are sometimes the targets of violence and are even killed simply because they're gay (or perceived to be gay).

Perhaps the most famous case of a person being murdered because he was gay happened in 1998, when Matthew Shepard, a student at the University of Wyoming, was brutally beaten by two young men who tied Matthew to a fence and left him to die. Matthew was found alive, but died several days later from his injuries. His murder, and the subsequent publicity, sparked nationwide protests against anti-gay violence and for anti-violence legislation. (There's a critically acclaimed play about the Matthew Shepard murder, called

The Laramie Project, which is often performed at high schools across the country. And HBO produced a movie based on the play.) (See Chapter 9, "Resources," for a complete list of movies and documentaries.)

✳ Why are lesbian and gay people who serve in the U.S. military forced to keep their sexual orientation a secret?

That's a good question. If you ask the people in charge of the U.S. military why they have these "Don't Ask, Don't Tell" rules, they'll tell you that they believe it would undermine morale and make it hard for soldiers to work as a team if gay people in the military didn't keep their sexual orientation a secret. But that hasn't been the experience in Canada, all Western European countries, and Israel. In these countries gay people in the military are not forced to keep their sexual orientation secret.

There have been many studies done about this issue, including some conducted by the U.S. military. All of these studies have shown that military and political leaders who don't want openly gay people to serve in the military are guided by prejudice and myths, not facts.

✳ How do countries around the world deal with gay and lesbian people?

In some places, gay people are treated no differently from anyone else and can live their lives the same as straight people do. In others, like Iran, where homosexual acts are illegal for both men and women and are punishable by death, gay people have to be very careful to keep their sexual orientation a secret.

In general, European countries have very liberal attitudes toward homosexuality and gay people are protected by law from discrimination. In other places around the world, particularly parts of Asia and Africa, gay and lesbian people often face great difficulties. But you really have to look at this issue country by country. For example, contrary to expectations, South Africa was the first nation in the world to write a constitution that included language banning discrimination against gay people.

✳ Are there organizations working for gay kids and teens?

Yes. There are currently hundreds of different organizations across the United States that provide a wide range of services for gay, lesbian, bisexual, and transgender youth, from peer counseling to education. These organizations are members of the National Youth Advocacy Coalition (NYAC), the largest national organization that works to improve the lives of these young people. In addition to working with many different organizations, NYAC focuses on social justice advocacy and health education. (See Chapter 9, "Resources," for more information.)

There are also thousands of schools in the United States that have GSAs (Gay-Straight Alliances) or other student groups for gay and lesbian students. This is the work of the Gay, Lesbian and Straight Education Network (GLSEN). The organization's goal is to make sure that "each member of every school community is valued and respected, regardless of sexual orientation." GLSEN's efforts include helping high school GSAs and working with education organizations to improve on what students are taught about homosexuality and gay people.

✳ What can young people do to make a difference?

Young people can do a lot, including speaking up in class as Erica and Mae did, telling friends not to use anti-gay language, asking your teacher to post a news bulletin board for stories on gay and lesbian issues, and starting or joining a GSA.

Several years back, six of Chris Lord's students decided to testify at state hearings in Maryland in favor of adding sexual orientation to a proposed anti-discrimination and hate crimes bill. Chris told me: "The six girls sat there for seven hours and all of them testified in front of the subcommittee in favor of the bill. They had done their research and did very well. This was an issue they felt strongly about."

Kevin is in eleventh grade at a suburban high school in

southern California. He's the president of his school's GSA, and thinks that one of the most important things for kids to do is to "break the cycle of hate." He explained, "There's a poem called 'Carefully Taught,' about how parents teach their children to hate, and their children teach *their* children to hate. If people understand that being gay is okay, that it's perfectly natural, it would be an easier environment for gay people to come out in. It would be better for everyone."

✳ What does the whole poem say?

It's actually not a poem, but the lyrics from a song, "You've Got to Be Carefully Taught," from the Broadway musical *South Pacific* by Richard Rodgers and Oscar Hammerstein II. The lyrics, which are as true today as they were when Hammerstein wrote them in 1949, talk about the responsibility adults bear for passing prejudice down from one generation to the next. Perhaps your generation will do better than generations past in making the world a more welcoming place for all people, no matter what their differences.

chapter 8
for parents

There is a lot written for parents who have gay children or think that their child might be gay, and that's the focus of this chapter (although there's also plenty here for people who simply want a better understanding of how they can talk to their children—or nieces and nephews or the other children in their lives—about gay people). But this chapter just scratches the surface, so if this is an important issue in your life, please think of this chapter as simply an introduction and then make use of the resources in Chapter 9 to become an expert, which is what you'll need to be if a child or young person you love is gay. (Also, if you haven't already, see the questions on coming out to parents in Chapter 2, "Friends and Family.")

✳ How do I talk to my children about gay people?

There's no particular time in the life of a child when you have to bring up the subject of gay people. It's likely to come up naturally if your child has a gay aunt or uncle or if there's something on television or in the news that catches a child's interest or sparks their curiosity. The challenge you're likely to face is how to respond to the comment or question in an age-appropriate way.

For example, I can remember like yesterday the panic in my sister's voice when I told her that my partner and I were having a commitment ceremony. "What," my sister asked, "am I going to say to Rachel?" Rachel (my sister's daughter, to whom this book happens to be dedicated) was eight years old at the time, and my sister had never talked to Rachel about the fact that Uncle Eric and Uncle Barney were gay and a couple.

Rachel knew my partner as Uncle Barney, but there had never been any discussion about the nature of our relationship during the year and a half that Barney and I had been together. Rachel had simply never asked any questions about us and seemed to take Uncle Barney and our relationship in stride. There had been no reason in the past to sit Rachel down and give her a lecture about homosexuality, and it's not what was called for now.

So I said to my sister, "Why don't you just tell Rachel

that Uncle Eric and Uncle Barney are having a ceremony like the wedding that Mommy and Daddy had"? Rachel happened to be right next to my sister while she was on the phone with me and I heard my sister turn to Rachel and repeat exactly what I'd said. And Rachel's response? First she wanted to know: "Is Uncle Eric going to move in to Uncle Barney's mansion?" Uncle Barney owned a New York City row house, which Rachel apparently thought was much bigger than a normal house. My sister said yes, which made Rachel happy because she'd been to Uncle Barney's house and really liked it. Then, without prompting, Rachel added (I could hear this over the phone): "Just tell Uncle Eric that I'm glad he's finally found a nice husband." My sister and I were speechless! Rachel got it, and no other explanations were required.

What I know terrified my sister (I know this because we've talked about it since, and I've also talked with lots of other parents who have found themselves in similar circumstances) was that she was somehow going to have to explain the nature of our physical relationship—that we were two guys who had sex with each other. So she panicked and forgot that she was talking to an eight-year-old and didn't need to get into such details. Besides which, that wasn't what Rachel wanted or needed to know.

Panic is what I've heard from parents over and over again when faced with a child's seemingly innocent question or comment, like a four-year-old who asks why his two aunts sleep in the same bed. The simple, age-appropriate answer is: "Because they love each other." Depending on the circumstances, you might elaborate and say: "Because they're married to each other like Mommy and Daddy and they love each other." And what if there's a follow-up question or statement like: "I didn't know that two girls could get married." Easy. The answer is, "Yes, they can." Do you have to explain the exact legal circumstances for gay couples in the state in which you live? No, not unless your child is old enough—and interested enough—to have a conversation about the social, political, and religious debate over extending legal marriage to same-sex couples. And even then, there are simple ways of having that conversation with a young child or teenager.

Children are also not beyond asking sex questions, like, "Do they have sex?" The simple answer is: "Yes. Gay people are just like everyone else." If there are further questions and you're too embarrassed and/or uncomfortable having that conversation, then hand them a copy of this book (assuming they're old enough to read it).

When panic sets in, or even before panic sets in, the way you talk to children about gay people is to consider how old the child is and then give an age-appropriate answer. I'm of the general belief that the simple answer is often the better answer, especially with very young children. If a child isn't satisfied with the simple answer, you'll get more questions later. And what if you don't have the answers? You can always say, "I'm not sure," and then do some research on your own or with your child to find the answer.

Sometimes it's a child's pejorative remark about gay people that presents an opportunity to start a conversation (as I write about in the last question in Chapter 1). That's what happened with Don and Stacy when their four boys started tossing around the phrase "that's so gay." Don asked his sons, most of whom were in middle school at the time, if they knew what "gay" meant. He told me: "They only had a vague sense, so my wife and I explained about how most men are attracted to women and some are attracted to men and that most women are attracted to men and some are attracted to women. I'm sure we didn't talk about the specifics regarding sexuality, but talked more in terms of emotion and closeness, and that if people are gay, it's because it's the essence of who they are."

Don added, "I also told them about our friends and our family members who are gay and dear to us. They'd met some of these people, so this wasn't something abstract. They were real human beings. I think prejudice comes out when it's an abstract issue. When you make it real it changes things."

Don and Stacy decided that it wasn't enough to talk to their boys in such broad terms, but they also knew that if they'd taken the conversation much further the boys would have been embarrassed into silence. Not certain of what to do, Stacy picked up one of my books at her bookstore (an adult version of this book, which is called *Is It a Choice?*) and then e-mailed me to ask if I had any suggestions about how to keep the conversation going without embarrassing all of them, parents included.

I suggested to Stacy, as I have to many parents, that she give this book to her sons to read. (This is something I also often recommend to young people who have come out to their parents but prefer not to personally answer their parents' questions.) Stacy and Don decided that it wasn't enough to just give a book to their sons. They made it a required reading assignment and after all of them had read it, they discussed it over dinner. "I think it really helped demystify the subject for them," Stacy reported in a follow-up e-mail.

✳ How can parents tell if their child is gay?

There's no way to tell for certain whether your child (or anyone, for that matter) is gay unless he or she tells you. You might have a hunch, but the only one who can confirm it is your child.

Lots of parents start wondering about their child's

sexual orientation if their child doesn't fit typical gender stereotypes. Your daughter might like playing soccer in her overalls; your son might play house instead of tackling other boys in the backyard. While it's true that a lot of kids who are gender atypical at young ages grow up to be gay, this is certainly not always the case.

That said, it's gender atypical behavior and other clues that often lead parents to think that a child might be gay. All of the parents I've heard from in recent years who have wanted to discern whether a child is gay have done so out of a desire to be the best parents they can to a gay child, not out of a wish to make the child straight—and that's the context in which I'm answering this question.

For Don and Stacy, who think that their youngest son, Kenny, is gay, it was Kenny's difference from his brothers that first made them wonder. Skiing has always been central to their family life and all four sons are accomplished athletes, but from early on, Kenny was still different from the others. Don explained, "From around the age of five . . . before Kenny became aware that it wasn't socially acceptable to do so, he dressed up in wigs and his mother's clothing. Early on, the other boys sensed he was different and started picking on him."

Now that the boys are older, Kenny's difference is far less obvious, although, unlike his brothers, whose rooms are covered with posters of female models, the walls of

Kenny's room are covered with *National Geographic* maps. "And it's not just that," adds Don. "Stacy and I are pretty smart, involved, and perceptive parents. There was a period when Kenny was very withdrawn and unhappy and we think that's when he was just beginning to struggle with questions about his sexuality. We sent him to a counselor, hoping that that would help, but he only went for a few sessions before telling us he didn't want to go anymore. That was a while ago now, and he still hasn't said anything to us about being gay, but he seems pretty happy and relaxed these days, and that's what's important to us."

Gail Beauchamp, who has three children and lives in northern Michigan, had a sense that her second child was gay from the time she was in middle school. "What first got our attention was her athleticism. But more than that, she wasn't interested in boys the way other girls were interested in boys. When other girls were beginning to dress provocatively to get their attention, Shannon did just the opposite, to cover up her figure with loose turtlenecks and baggy jeans. She hung out with boys, but they were her friends."

Genny had a sense that her son, Devon, was different when he was very young. "When he was ten months old we took him to have his picture taken and we decided to bring some props—a bat and a ball. Turns out, he didn't give a crap about baseball. When he was eighteen months old we took him for another photograph and surrounded him with books. He loved books and still loves books. But what he really loved were dolls. When he was three or four we'd go into a toy store and he'd go right for the Barbie dolls. We didn't panic, but his father and I thought it was interesting and talked about it being a possibility down the line that one day he might be gay."

Devon is now fourteen, and Genny is virtually certain that he's gay. She explained, "If he talks about girls—and all of his friends are girls—he never talks about them the way other boys do. He might notice their figure flaws, but it's not at all sexual. He hates sports and is totally into the arts—he won't even ride his bicycle. Let me tell you, if Devon turns out to be straight and marries a girl, it will be the shock of my life. And I'll be a little disappointed, because I think I'd have a hard time sharing him with another woman."

* My eleven-year-old son told me he thinks he's gay. Isn't that too young for him to know? What should I say?

I know people who figured out they were gay before they had a word for it—guys who recall having serious crushes on boys at age five, and if you look back, you might recall having crushes on people of the opposite sex that early too. And these days kids are far more likely to have a word for their feelings than when I was growing up. So it's no longer surprising for me when I get an e-mail from an eleven-year-old asking me how she can talk to her parents about being gay.

If your child is telling you he's gay, believe him—he's the best expert on this subject—and don't try to persuade him otherwise. If it turns out that he's not gay, he'll let you know when he figures that out. The key is to avoid giving any indication that you're upset or confused. You're the parent, and what a child is looking for in this circumstance is reassurance. Save your upset or confusion for a discussion with your spouse and/or a counselor (see the next question for more information).

On occasion I've heard from parents who were unsure what to say when a young child expressed confusion about whether he or she might be gay. I like what one father told me was his response to his young son who asked him if he thought he was gay: "He asked me what I thought. I told him that I didn't know if he was gay, but that he would come to understand this about himself as he got older. And I also told him, 'This is not something you need to worry about, and your mother and I will always love you.' I also told him that when he fell in love, that we would love that person too, whether that person was a girl or a boy."

✳ My teenage child has just come out to me. What should I do? What should I say?

Listen and be supportive. It was probably not easy for your child to bring this up, and she probably did so because she cares about you and wants to be honest with you (which is a tribute to your relationship with her). Make sure you let her know that you appreciate this and that you love and support her no matter what. While the news might take some getting used to, your first concern should be making sure your child doesn't feel she has disappointed or upset you.

That said, you're probably grappling with some of your own concerns, including a sense of loss (for the future you had imagined for your child) or disappointment, but try not to share your concerns with your child. She's probably feeling sensitive about your reactions, and hearing your worries may only add to her own. That's unfortunately what happened when Shane came out to her father. She said, "He started crying and telling me how he thought this wasn't normal, that it wasn't what he wanted for me."

Sometime later, Shane's father told a friend how he reacted to Shane's coming out. "He explained to the friend that he'd been crying and openly expressing his dismay and really indulging his feelings in front of me," Shane said. "He later shared with me that the friend said something to him that snapped things back into perspective for him and he realized, 'Wow, that must have been really hard for Shane.'"

It wasn't until Shane's dad told her about his experience of talking with his friend that she realized she didn't have to simply accept her father's behavior. She said, "Up until then, it hadn't dawned on me that I didn't have to completely indulge my father's feelings. I just thought I had to sit there and take it because at least he wasn't yelling and he was still talking to me." Shane and her dad now joke about that first coming out conversation, which Shane likes to call his "meltdown."

Shane would have been better off if her dad had contained his emotions and shared with a friend or family member how upset he was, but that's often easier said than done. And not everyone is comfortable talking to people they know about such a potentially sensitive subject.

If you find yourself in a situation like Shane's dad (or even if you're just confused and need to sort out your feelings), consider seeing a counselor for a session or two. I also suggest that you contact Parents, Families and Friends of Lesbians and Gays (see Chapter 9, "Resources," for more details about PFLAG), where you can meet and talk to other parents who have been down the same road.

✳ I think my daughter/son may be gay. Should I ask? If she/he is, why hasn't she/he talked to me?

Some young people want to be asked. I did, and I dropped enough hints until, finally, my mother asked me if I was gay, and I said yes. On the other hand, if your child is still working through her feelings, she may be doing everything she can to hide the truth from herself and from you and would not likely be open to your questions. And even if she has worked through her feelings and is sure that she's gay, she may hold back from telling you for fear that she'll disappoint or upset you. If your child has heard you make anti-gay remarks or knows that you hold strict religious beliefs, she may be especially reluctant to be truthful about her sexual orientation—and with good reason. So even if you ask, you may not get an honest answer.

Gail Beauchamp was tempted to ask her daughter, Shannon, if she was gay, especially after Shannon said that people at work were saying things about her being a lesbian. "She was a senior in high school then and I wondered if she was trying to get me to talk about it with her, but I wasn't smart enough to pick up on it. Also, I didn't want to risk insulting her." There was one other thing that kept Gail from asking. During high school Shannon dated a boy for more than a year, which left Gail and her husband confused. Gail explained: "When Shannon first introduced her boyfriend to us, that really threw us for a loop. My husband and I talked about how it wasn't what we'd expected. So I thought it was better not to say anything and just waited for Shannon to talk to me if she wanted."

Because it's difficult to know for sure whether your

child is gay—and asking directly can be a real conversation stopper—one approach for beginning a conversation is for *you* to drop the hints that this is a subject you're comfortable with. If your child is considering coming out to you, chances are she's looking for clues that you'll respond positively and will notice if you drop some.

For example, if you read a news story about a gay-related issue, or if a gay character appears on a TV show or in a movie you're watching, try discussing it. If you have gay friends or family members, talk about them with your child in a positive way. And since you're reading this book, you might try offering it to your child, or leaving it where she can find it.

✳ So what is the right time to ask?

There is no ideal or right time that suits every circumstance. So here are just a few examples from people you've already met in this chapter.

Genny thinks that it's still too soon to ask her fourteen-year-old son, who has given her every reason to believe that dating girls is not in his future. "If Devon were talking about it, I'd be on it in a second. I try to get a sense of his mind-set and sometimes ask him something about other kids dating, but it's not what's he interested in talking about right now."

Genny thinks that if Devon hasn't brought it up himself by the time he's sixteen, she'll raise the subject of his sexual orientation. She explained, "I think it really depends on the kid and right now it feels like sixteen would be the right age. Look, what's important to me is Devon's happiness. His father and I don't want this to be a burden to him, especially since it's not an issue for us. We're crazy about him, in case you couldn't tell."

Don and Stacy go back and forth about when would be the right time to talk to Kenny and are hoping he raises the subject sooner rather than later. If he doesn't, they've decided they'll bring it up before he leaves for college. Don said, "We might sit him down and bring it up directly. My hope is that it would liberate him a little, that this big secret he may have doesn't have to be a secret. I think it might make things easier for him if we're able to talk about it."

Don and Stacy have already made clear to their children how they feel about gay people, so they know that if Kenny is in fact struggling with his sexuality he won't have to worry that his parents will do anything other than embrace him.

With Gail Beauchamp, the opening to talk to her daughter came when Shannon brought home one of her friends (the boyfriend was out of the picture by then). "Her friend fit the look," Gail explained, "bandanna around her head, baggy T-shirt—it was a boy look. Later that day Shannon and I were driving somewhere and Shannon told me that her friend was gay and she hoped I didn't have a problem with that. I said to Shannon that I kind of figured she was and that that was okay with me. And then I added,

'If you are, that's okay too.'" Shannon gave Gail a slightly stunned look, and Gail told her, "I love you."

The fact that her daughter is gay (and now in a relationship with a woman) is not an issue for Gail. "All I care about," she said, "is that my children pick people who are good to them. It's not a gender thing. It's not a color thing. It's a treatment thing. I'm happy that Shannon gets along with her partner and that they treat each other well."

✳ What can I do to protect gay children against discrimination (my own kids, my nieces and nephews, etc.)?

Talk about it. One on one. With your friends, with your family. I'm convinced after the many years that I've been writing and talking about gay people that the only way change happens—the only way to end discrimination—is when someone who is close to the subject (like a gay person or a family member) speaks up, whether it's in a casual conversation with other parents about one's child or in a political discussion about pending legislation that affects gay people.

From the day she learned that her daughter was gay, Gail Beauchamp has never hesitated to speak up when she hears something she doesn't like, whether what she hears comes from a colleague complaining about "faggots" or from someone in her Bible study group. "We had the first meeting at my house a week ago," Gail explained, "and this topic came up. It was a perfect opportunity. I said, 'Okay, I have a daughter who lives with her boyfriend, and a daughter who lives with her girlfriend. Am I supposed to *not* have the girlfriend come over but it's okay to have the boyfriend come over?' I said that we're supposed to be accepting and loving and kind. We talked for quite a while about it, but the bottom line was that everyone agreed with me."

Before Gail started talking to other people about her daughter being gay, she asked Shannon if it was okay for her to do so, which it was. "I didn't want to do it without asking," Gail said, "because I didn't want to step on her toes." Now that she's free to talk, Gail thinks that sometimes she's too outspoken, "but the way I feel, I can't not say something. I've talked with other parents in the past and they think it's totally crazy and say they would have nothing to do with their kid if they were gay and I say, 'I hope your child never has to deal with that.' I just don't understand that. So I feel an obligation to speak up. We need to accept everyone for who they are." Gail added, "My daughter thinks I'm going to become this big activist." It seems to me that Gail has already made a running start.

✳ Do you have any examples from your own family?

Yes, my uncle is a good example of someone who has chosen to speak up and he does it with two of his buddies from Brooklyn College, whom he's known for years. They talk about all kinds of issues and inevitably follow up their initial discussions with e-mail debates. Having become something of an expert on the subject of gay people, my uncle is quick to argue his case (my case), whether the subject is gay people serving in the military or extending legal marriage to gay couples.

My uncle didn't become an expert overnight, and it took years before he was comfortable making full-throated arguments, but over time he's grown into his role among his friends as the one who can be counted on to stand on the side of gay civil rights. And I like to think that he's helped shift a few opinions along the way.

Another way you can make yourself heard and let other people know what you're thinking is to write a letter to your local elected official or congressperson when there's pending legislation that you agree—or disagree—with. (Given how many e-mails politicians receive these days, I think it's more effective to hand-write and send a letter through the mail.) And you can call, too. It doesn't hurt to register your opinion in more than one way, especially since politicians keep track of these things (and one can hope that what you say will have an impact on that politician's thinking and voting decisions).

You can also write a letter to your local newspaper in response to something you've read. You never know whom you'll reach that way, whether it's another parent (who is more likely to listen to another parent than to someone like me) or a young gay person, who may be inspired or encouraged by your words. For example, I remember going on a trip to Boston back in 1993 to give a talk to a group of gay business-people. I was reading the editorial page of the *New York Times* and was surprised by a headline in the "Letters" column, which read: "Parents of Gays." Under it was a single letter in response to an op-ed piece written by Paul Monette, a well-known author and gay activist, who has since died from AIDS.

I thought it was a great letter from a parent who clearly loved her child, and then I jumped out of my seat when I got to the end of the letter and saw that it was *my* mother who had written it! Mom didn't tell me about the letter, having decided in advance that she would let me be surprised in the event it was published. It was, and *I* was! Here's what the letter said:

> To the Editor:
> As the proud mother of a gay son, I would salute Paul Monette for "The Politics of Silence" (Op-Ed March 7). Parents go through intensive consciousness-raising when their child comes out. For all of us have internalized the bigotry and self-limited thinking of society's homophobia. In time, we learn that our sons and daughters are the same people we have always loved and known.

> Above all, we want our children to have full and expressive
> lives, to be treated with respect and protected by the civil
> laws of our country. The time has come for families to be
> seen and heard.
> CECILIA MARCUS
> New York, March 15, 1993

Beyond talking and writing, you can also give financial support to an organization like GLSEN (Gay, Lesbian and Straight Education Network) or PFLAG (Parents, Families and Friends of Lesbians and Gays) or contact one of these organizations and find out how you can help in a meaningful way in your community. Only you can decide what's comfortable for you. But the key is to *do* something. Each and every one of us can make a difference, but not if we remain silent and on the sidelines.

✳ My child is getting called names at school because he/she is perceived to be gay. What can I do?

You can start by doing what you ought to do anytime a child is teased or bullied: Let him know you love him and that he doesn't deserve to be treated this way. Virtually no child, gay or straight, gets through school without being picked on for one reason or another, so you can rest assured— unfortunately—that you and your child are not alone.

You probably can't help but wonder if the reason your child is being teased is *because* he is gay. But if he hasn't chosen this moment—when he's feeling particularly vulnerable—to come out to you, then don't force the issue. Avoiding that question lets him know that the teasing is wrong whether he's gay or not.

Although every circumstance is different, what you most likely need to do is make an appointment to speak with your child's guidance counselor or the school principal. Provide a detailed, written report of the incident that includes names and dates. Offer concrete suggestions—for example, if the bullying has happened on more than one occasion in the same place, such as the gym locker room, request increased supervision in that area. Follow up to find out what is being done to address your concerns, and if you don't get a satisfying response, go to the superintendent or the school board. Make sure you're aware of your school's and state's policies—a few states have laws that specifically protect students from anti-gay bullying and harassment.

Beyond your child's school, there are resources that you can call on, both for bullying in general and more specifically for anti-gay bullying. For example, you can look to GLSEN or other local or national resources for suggestions about how to help your child deal with bullying and to learn about programs and curricula that you can recommend to your child's school. (See the next question and

Chapter 9, "Resources," for more information.)

Jennie, who is a guidance counselor at a high school in a suburban school district outside New York City, learned in a roundabout way about how her son Stephen was being teased. "When Stephen was in seventh grade, one night I went into his room to kiss him good night and I could tell something was wrong. So I asked him what was going on. Fortunately, he's a pretty verbal kid and he asked me, 'How does somebody know if they're gay?'"

Knowing that there was something behind the question, Jennie asked Stephen why he was asking the question in the first place. She explained: "He told me that some of the kids at school were calling him gay and he couldn't understand why. He knew what gay meant, but it wasn't how he thought of himself."

Jennie and her husband had talked many times as Stephen was growing up about the possibility that he might be gay, so the question didn't come as a shock. "We talked about it a lot and how we felt about it," she explained. "We knew there was nothing we could do about it, so knowing that this was how it was going to be, our goal was 'How can we make it as easy for him as we can?'"

As Jennie saw things in that moment in her son's bedroom, the first challenge was to put Stephen at ease about his sexuality, which Jennie did by telling him that he might not know for a while whether he was gay, but that he'd come to understand his feelings more clearly as he got older. And then they talked about how he could deal with the teasing, which was coming primarily from another boy. "Stephen's preference was to simply ignore the name-calling," Jennie said, "but the teasing didn't stop, so later we talked about another tactic, which was to confront the boy doing the teasing by saying 'Yes, I'm so happy, what about you?'"

Around the time Jennie and her son had this second conversation and before Stephen had the chance to try confronting the classmate on his own, a teacher who had overheard the teasing reported it to the school's dean, who called Stephen and his tormentor in for a meeting. "I will tell you," explained Jennie, "that as uncomfortable as it was for Stephen to go to the dean's office and to partici- pate in a mediation with that kid, it stopped the teasing."

In tenth grade Stephen spoke to his mom again about the possibility that he was gay, Jennie recalled, "but it wasn't until he came back from college for his first Thanks- giving after leaving home that he told us that he was in fact gay. This was always fine with us and we were just glad that Stephen was comfortable with himself."

✱ Are there anti-bullying resources you can recommend?

As any parent knows, bullying is a problem that's hardly restricted to gay kids or kids perceived to be gay. So there are plenty of resources out there, including these three helpful websites:

www.safeyouth.org contains information and resources for teens being bullied,

www.bullycoach.com is a great resource for parents and teachers who are looking for advice and information on how to intervene in cases of bullying,

www.safeschoolscoalition.org offers information specifically about anti-gay bullying.

✻ How do I talk to other parents about my gay child?

If you're not comfortable talking about your gay child, then you might choose to avoid talking about it altogether. This will most likely be easier when your child is younger, but more difficult when he or she grows up and is dating or has settled down with a same-sex partner.

If you want to talk honestly with other parents about your child, then I suggest doing so as matter-of-factly as you would talk about a straight child. If you speak with shame, people will respond with embarrassment and/or by feeling sorry for you. If you talk about it like it's not a big deal and with a sense of pride, it's more likely that your friends—assuming they don't have strong anti-gay beliefs—will respond in kind.

My mother really struggled with this in the years before all of her many cousins knew that I was gay (my mother was an only child, but grew up in a large immigrant family). Mom had one experience early on in her own coming-out process (coming out about being the mother of a gay son) that really shook her up, but also made her more determined that she wasn't going to hide.

The incident took place at a family Thanksgiving, which I did not attend, shortly after my first book was published. I knew my mom well enough to know that she probably struggled between her pride over her son having published a book and her fear of how her cousins might react to the subject of the book, which was a guide for male couples. Pride ultimately won out, and midway through dinner, Mom produced a copy of the book and handed it to one cousin, who handed it to another cousin.

The book made it around the entire table with a comment from only one cousin, a comment that included the word "faggot." In telling me about the experience, I could tell that my mother was humiliated, embarrassed, and furious, but ultimately emboldened. And over time she got to the point where she never hesitated to mention that her son was gay, had a partner, and that he wrote books about gay people. I know that this wasn't easy for her at first, but a parent's love for a child—her love for me—beat out whatever nervousness she might have had about what people might think of her. Or me. I was very proud of my mom and I think that she set a fine example for all parents who have gay children.

✳ Is it okay for my kids to play with kids who have gay parents?

Yes. For more information, see the last few questions of Chapter 3, "Dating, Marriage, and Kids."

✳ My brother/sister is gay. Will he/she be a bad influence on my children?

No. If anything, your brother or sister can be a *good* influence. Chances are, having a gay aunt or uncle will help your child to be open-minded and accepting of difference. I like to think that that's been the experience of my niece and two nephews. Having grown up with my partner and me as their uncles, they seem unself-conscious about the subject of gay people, and my niece has become something of an expert. And that's not a recent occurrence.

When my niece was all of thirteen, she called to ask me if I could take her to a huge gay rights march that was planned for Washington, D.C., in 2000. I hadn't planned to go, but I couldn't say no to my niece, who, during the parade, very gamely fielded questions from a group of older lesbians who were curious to know why she wanted to be at the march. Rachel explained that she thought it was important to stand up and be counted in the fight for equal rights.

✳ Where can I get more information specifically for parents?

Parents, Families and Friends of Lesbians and Gays (PFLAG) is a nonprofit organization with hundreds of chapters and affiliates around the United States (and some overseas as well). By becoming a member and getting involved, you can meet other parents of gay people. Their website (www.pflag.org) has information about helpful books and has suggestions for how to get involved, how to start your own chapter if there isn't one nearby, and how to find other organizations for parents of gay and lesbian children.

For additional resources, including a list of books that provide far more information than I can in this book, please turn to the next chapter.

chapter 9
resources

A re you looking for someone to talk to? Help with a problem? Ideas on how to start a Gay-Straight Alliance at your school? A telephone number for a gay youth group in your area? A telephone hotline? A book or video? Help with a religious question? Then you've come to the right place. All of the information you're looking for is out there, and the resources in this section will help you find it.

Before you check out any of the websites I recommend, please read the following:

You'll see that virtually all of the organizations I list have a website. That means that if you have access to the Internet, you can get enormous amounts of information and help online. You can also purchase the books and DVDs/videos I list through a commercial website (and sometimes directly through the organizations).

But as I already said in the introduction to Chapter 1—and it bears repeating here—it's extremely important to be cautious when you use the Internet, especially if you decide to join a discussion group or use the Internet to meet other young people. Because it's so easy to create a false online profile, it can be hard to tell who is being truthful and who is not. So there's the possibility that someone may try to take advantage of you, may make you uncomfortable online, or might try to arrange to meet you when they should not. Always remember that when meeting people online, you should use the same caution you would when meeting any stranger. Never give out your telephone number or home address, and never agree to meet anyone in person unless you are accompanied by a parent or another responsible adult—and then only meet in a public place.

The Internet is an amazing resource, but I urge you to be careful and to use common sense when you go online. And, if possible, please seek guidance from your parents or a responsible adult.

✳ Nonfiction Books

***Prayers for Bobby: A Mother's Coming to Terms
with the Suicide of Her Gay Son,*** **by Leroy Aarons.
Harper-SanFrancisco, 1996.**

Author Leroy Aarons traces Mary Griffith's struggle to reconcile her teenage son's sexuality, his suicide, and her own religious beliefs. (Not written specifically for young adults.)

***Free Your Mind: The Book for Gay, Lesbian, and
Bisexual Youth and Their Allies,*** **by Ellen Bass and
Kate Kaufman. HarperCollins, 1996.**

Free Your Mind offers practical advice and information for young gay, lesbian, and bisexual people as well as their families, teachers, counselors, and friends.

Am I Blue? Coming Out from the Silence; **Marion Dane Bauer, editor. Trophy Press, 1995.**

This American Library Association award-winning anthology includes sixteen funny, sad, and memorable short stories for teens about coming out as gay or lesbian.

Passages of Pride: Lesbian and Gay Youth Come of Age, **by Kurt Chandler. Times Books, 1995.**

Six teenagers speak of the challenges they faced growing up, coming out, and making peace at home, at school, and on their own.

Queer 13: Lesbian and Gay Writers Recall Seventh Grade;
Clifford Chase, editor. Rob Weisbach Books, 1999.

Queer 13 includes twenty-five stories written by a range of writers who offer various points of view about their teen years.

The Family Heart: A Memoir of When Our Son Came
Out, by Robb Forman Dew. Addison-Wesley, 1994.

I recommend this one for parents.

Two Teenagers in Twenty: Writings by Gay and Lesbian
Youth; Ann Heron, editor. Alyson Books, 1994.

Forty-two people between the ages of twelve and twenty-four describe how they came to realize they were gay, how they explained their sexual orientation to their families and friends, and how their lives have been affected by their sexuality.

Becoming Visible: A Reader in Gay and Lesbian History
for High School and College Students; Kevin Jennings,
editor. Alyson Books, 1994.

The selections included here cover more than two thousand years of history and a diverse range of cultures. Questions and suggestions for classroom activities follow at the end of each section.

Does Your Mama Know? An Anthology of Black
Lesbian Coming Out Stories; Lisa C. Moore,
editor. Redbone Press, 1998.

The complex emotions that accompany coming out are captured in forty-nine short stories, poems, interviews, and essays. (Not written specifically for young adults, but appropriate for high school students.)

✳ Fiction Books

Annie on My Mind, by Nancy Garden. Farrar, Strauss and Giroux, 1982.

Seventeen-year-old Liza's friendship with Annie turns into a love relationship. Once discovered, they must find the strength to stay together.

Boy Meets Boy, by David Levithan. Knopf Books for Young Readers, 2005.

Author David Levithan introduces readers to an engaging cast of characters who attend an ideal high school where kids get to be themselves without fear of being teased or ostracized.

Luna, by Julie Anne Peters. Little, Brown Young Readers, 2004.

Regan is fiercely protective of her transgender brother, who is Liam by day and Luna by night. According to the *School Library Journal*, *Luna* is "a sensitive and poignant portrayal of a young man's determination to live his true identity."

Rainbow Boys, *Rainbow High*, and *Rainbow Road*, by Alex Sanchez. Simon & Schuster, 2003–2007.

This trilogy, written by one of my favorite novelists, follows three gay friends through their senior year in high school and after.

Getting It, **by Alex Sanchez. Simon & Schuster, 2006.**
Fifteen-year-old Carlos asks Sal, the gay guy at school, to make him over so he can stop being a "girlfriend-less virgin." Sal agrees, in exchange for Carlos's help with forming a Gay-Straight Alliance.

So Hard to Say, **by Alex Sanchez.**
Simon & Schuster, 2004.
Newly arrived in California, eighth grader Frederick meets and becomes friends with a girl who develops a major crush on him, but their relationship takes an awkward turn because he's attracted to a boy.

Letters in the Attic, **by Bonnie Shimko.**
Academy Chicago, 2002.
Set in the 1960s, a young girl moves with her unstable mother from Arizona to upstate New York and finds herself falling for another girl, an eighth grader who "looks like Natalie Wood and smokes."

Growing Up Gay/Growing Up Lesbian: A Literary Anthology;
Bennett L. Singer, editor. The New Press, 1994.
More than fifty prominent lesbian and gay writers and scholars have contributed coming-of-age and coming-out stories to this anthology.

A Really Nice Prom Mess, **by Brian Sloan.**
Simon & Schuster, 2005.
Author Brian Sloan chronicles the outrageous prom night

and the morning after of a gay high school senior on a double date with a redheaded bombshell beauty instead of his football star boyfriend.

A Tale of Two Summers, by Brian Sloan.
Simon & Schuster, 2006.

Lifelong best friends—one gay, one straight—are spending the summer apart and share their experiences of discovery on their private blog.

Not the Only One: Lesbian and Gay Fiction for Teens;
Jane Summer, editor. Alyson Books, 2004.

This anthology about friendship, family, and love deals with coming-of-age themes such as leaving home, falling in love, and confronting secrets.

From the Notebooks of Melanin Sun,
by Jacqueline Woodson. Scholastic, 1997.

When his mother announces that she's gay, a fourteen-year-old African-American boy has to decide what to do. Winner of the 1996 Coretta Scott King Honor Book Award, James Addams Peace Award, and American Library Association Best Book for Young Adults.

✳ Books on Sexuality

Changing Bodies, Changing Lives, by Ruth Bell.
Random House, 1981.

This comprehensive encyclopedia of teen sexuality covers

everything from the physical and emotional aspects of puberty and sexually transmitted diseases to safer sex and birth control.

***It's Perfectly Normal: Changing Bodies, Growing Up, Sex, and Sexual Health*, by Robie H. Harris. Candlewick Press, 2004.**

In this frank, intelligent, and accessible illustrated book, author Robie Harris explains the physical, psychological, emotional, and social changes that occur during puberty and their implications.

***Doing It Right: Making Smart, Safe, and Satisfying Choices About Sex*, by Bronwen Pardes. Simon and Schuster, 2007.**

Required reading for every teen, *Doing It Right* tells young people just about everything they need to know about sex and sexuality, in an accessible, warm, and engaging way.

✳ DVDs/Videos

***All God's Children*, produced by Woman Vision, The National Gay and Lesbian Task Force, and The National Black Lesbian and Gay Leadership Forum; 26 minutes; 1996.**

All God's Children chronicles the Black Church's acceptance of African-American lesbian and gay people. Includes classroom study guide.

***Both of My Moms' Names are Judy*, produced by Lesbian and Gay Parents Association; 11 minutes; 1994.**

Children ages 7–11 candidly discuss their families, playground teasing, and classroom silence. Presenter's guide included.

Gay Youth, **produced by Pam Walton; 40 minutes; 1995.**
Gay Youth details the lives of two young people, showing that information, acceptance, and support can make an enormous difference to lesbian and gay youth.

Growing Up Gay and Lesbian; **57 minutes; 1993.**
Brian McNaught puts a powerful face on this issue with a nonthreatening but highly effective presentation on the isolation and alienation of growing up gay.

I Just Want to Say, **produced by GLSEN; 13 minutes; 1998.**
A panel of parents, students, and teachers talk about anti-gay bias in schools. Hosted by Martina Navratilova.

It's Elementary, **by Debra Chasnoff and Helen Cohen; 78 minutes; 1995.**
Inspiring footage shot in schools across the country shows real examples of school activities, faculty meetings, and classroom discussions of lesbian, gay, bisexual, and trans-gender issues. Includes classroom study guide.

The Laramie Project, **produced by HBO; 97 minutes; 2002.**
Based on the nonfiction play by Moisés Kaufman, this is the true story of the people of Laramie, Wyoming, following the murder of gay college student Matthew Shepard.

Out of the Past, **by Jeff Dupre; 60 minutes; 1998.**
Through the eyes of a young woman coming to terms

with herself and her place in the world, *Out of the Past* traces the emergence of gay men and lesbians in American history.

***Straight from the Heart*, produced by Woman Vision; 25 minutes; 1994.**

This video contains the stories of parents and their journeys to a new understanding of their lesbian, gay, and bisexual children. Includes a classroom study guide.

✳ National Organizations—General

There are organizations across the country working on different aspects of the gay civil rights movement. The following groups work at the national level, and each maintains a website containing information about the work of the organization. Their websites may also include extensive resource listings, online newsletters, libraries, and contact information for local organizations.

GLAAD (Gay and Lesbian Alliance Against Defamation)

Since the mid-1980s, GLAAD has worked to make certain that the various media (including television, magazines, newspapers, and film) do a fair and accurate job of portraying gay, lesbian, bisexual, and transgender people.

GLAAD

212-807-1700

800-GAY-MEDIA

www.glaad.org

glaad@glaad.org

HRC (Human Rights Campaign)

The Human Rights Campaign is the largest national lesbian and gay political organization in the country. HRC lobbies the federal government on gay and AIDS-related issues; educates the public; participates in election campaigns; organizes volunteers; and provides help to state and local groups that work for gay and lesbian equal rights.

Human Rights Campaign

202-628-4160

www.hrc.org

hrc@hrc.org

Lambda Legal Defense and Education Fund

Lambda takes on a wide range of legal cases concerning the civil rights of lesbians, gay men, and people with HIV/AIDS. Their website provides extensive information on current and past efforts on topics ranging from the Boy Scouts to Gay-Straight Alliances.

Lambda Legal Defense and Education Fund

212-809-8585

www.lambdalegal.org

lambdalegal@lambdalegal.org

NGLTF (National Gay and Lesbian Task Force)

NGLTF works with local and state organizations to help them with their efforts in the gay and lesbian civil rights movement.

NGLTF

202-332-6483

www.thetaskforce.org

ngltf@ngltf.org

PFLAG (Parents, Families and Friends of Lesbians and Gays)

PFLAG is a support, education, and advocacy organization with chapters across the United States and around the world. If you would like to talk to an understanding parent or need specific advice on how to deal with your parents, contact your local PFLAG chapter.

PFLAG

202-638-4200

www.pflag.org

info@pflag.org

✳ National Organizations—Young People

There are hundreds of local groups and organizations across the country for gay, lesbian, bisexual, and transgender young people and their allies. The organizations I've listed below are some of the national groups (including COLAGE, which is specifically for the children of gay and lesbian people). If you want to locate a group in your area, check out the websites of these organizations and also have a look at the listings under "Websites," later in this chapter.

COLAGE (Children of Lesbians and Gays Everywhere)

COLAGE is a support and advocacy organization for the daughters and sons of lesbian, gay, bisexual, and transgender parents.

COLAGE

415-861-5437

www.colage.org

colage@colage.org

GLSEN (Gay, Lesbian and Straight Education Network)

GLSEN works to make sure that each member of every school community is valued and respected, regardless of sexual orientation. The organization's website offers extensive resources for teachers and students.

GLSEN

212-727-0135

www.glsen.org

glsen@glsen.org

NYAC (National Youth Advocacy Coalition)

NYAC advocates for and with young people who are lesbian, gay, bisexual, or transgender in an effort to end discrimination. Through NYAC, you can find information on gay youth groups in your area.

NYAC

202-319-7596 • 202-319-7365

www.nyacyouth.org

nyac@nyacyouth.org

Gay-Straight Alliance Network

This is a youth-led organization that connects school GSAs to one another and to community resources, and helps young people start and maintain GSAs in their schools.

GSA Network

415-552-4229

www.gsanetwork.org

info@gsanetwork.org

Advocates for Youth

Advocates for Youth helps young people make informed

and responsible decisions about their sexual health. Their website provides extensive information on all aspects of sexuality, with lots of resources and support for gay, lesbian, bisexual, and transgender teens.

Advocates for Youth

202-347-5700

www.advocatesforyouth.org

✳ Religious Organizations

There are religious organizations and groups for gay, lesbian, bisexual, and transgender people in local communities around the country. And hundreds of congregations from across the religious spectrum specifically welcome gay and lesbian people (they are a part of what's called the "Welcoming Congregation" movement).

In this section you'll find many of the national and umbrella religious groups, most of which provide contact information for local congregations.

American Baptists

The Association of Welcoming & Affirming Baptists

508-226-1945

www.WABaptists.org

WABaptists@aol.com

Episcopal
Integrity
> 202-462-9193
>
> www.integrityusa.org
>
> info@integrityusa.org

Jewish
World Congress of Gay, Lesbian, and Bisexual Jewish Organizations
> 202-452-7424
>
> www.glbtjews.org
>
> info@wcgljo.org

Lutheran
Lutherans Concerned North America
Includes members of all Lutheran denominations in North America.
> 404-266-9615
>
> www.lcna.org
>
> LuthConc@aol.com

Methodist
Affirmation
United Methodists for Lesbian, Gay, Bisexual & Transgender Concerns
> 847-733-9590

www.umaffirm.org

umaffirmation@yahoo.com

Mormon
Affirmation

323-255-7251

www.affirmation.org

Muslim
Al-Fatiha Foundation

212-752-3188

www.al-fatiha.org

info@al-fatiha.org

Roman Catholic
Dignity/USA

202-861-0017

www.dignityusa.org

dignity@aol.com

Unitarian Universalist Association of Congregations
Unitarian Universalists Office for Lesbian, Gay, Bisexual and Transgender Concerns

617-742-2100, ext. 475

www.uua.org/obgltc

obgltc@uua.org

Universal Fellowship of Metropolitan

Community Churches (MCC)

Universal Fellowship of Metropolitan Community

Churches

310-360-8640

www.ufmcc.com

info@mccchurch.net

✳ Websites

In addition to the websites maintained by the many organizations I've already listed earlier in this chapter, I'm including in this section a handful of websites specifically for young people who are interested in gay and lesbian issues, sexuality in general, and/or are looking for other young people to talk with online (please see my warning about the Internet at the beginning of the chapter before checking out any of these websites).

www.outproud.org

OutProud is the website for The National Coalition for Gay, Lesbian, Bisexual & Transgender Youth. The site offers a wide range of resources for young people and educators, including informational brochures, message boards, and coming-out stories. OutProud also publishes the QueerAmerica database (see next listing).

www.queeramerica.com

Just type in the first three numbers of your local phone number and the first three numbers of your zip code and the QueerAmerica database will provide a list of all the gay, lesbian, and bisexual resources in your area, including community centers, support organizations, PFLAG chapters, youth groups, and more. Other search alternatives offer access to organizations across the country.

www.youth-guard.org

This site is run by Youth Guardian Services, Inc., a youth-run nonprofit organization that provides support services on the Internet for gay, lesbian, bisexual, transgender, questioning, and straight, supportive youth. The site offers e-mail discussion groups for different age categories.

www.youthresource.com

Of all the websites for youths, www.youthresource.com is the most complete. Maintained by Advocates for Youth, a national organization based in Washington, D.C., this site offers online brochures, specific information for youth of color, advice on how to explore the Internet and chat online, recommended videos and books, information on HIV, news, Listservs for different age groups (once you subscribe, you can participate in discussions), and advice on how to start a Gay-Straight Alliance at your school.

www.teenwire.com

Planned Parenthood runs this sexual health website for teens. This is a great place to find out information and ask experts questions that you might have.

www.hivgettested.org
www.knowhivaids.org

These two websites will give you information on HIV/AIDS and will help you find places near you where you can get tested.

✳ Telephone Hotlines

Counseling, Information, Referrals
Gay & Lesbian National Hotline

Peer counseling, general information, and referrals.

888-THE-GLNH (888-843-4564)

www.glnh.org

glnh@glnh.org

Crisis Intervention
The Trevor Helpline

Nationwide, twenty-four-hour crisis helpline for lesbian, gay, bisexual, transgender, and questioning youth.

866-4U-TREVOR (866-488-7386)

www.thetrevorproject.org

support@thetrevorproject.org

HIV/AIDS and Sexually Transmitted Diseases
National AIDS Hotline

800-342-AIDS

GMHC (Gay Men's Health Crisis)

GMHC runs the nation's oldest and largest HIV hotline, which serves everyone, male or female, gay or straight. In addition to answering your questions over the telephone, you can request free written information on HIV, as well as referrals to local health facilities for testing and treatment.

1-800-AIDS-NYC

www.gmhc.org

National STD Hotline

This hotline provides information on STDs and how to prevent them. It also offers referrals for testing and treatment.

800-227-8922

SPECIAL ACKNOWLEDGMENT

O ne of the joys of growing older is the opportunity to see the children of your friends grow up. With Bronwen Pardes, I've had that opportunity, but even better, Bronwen and I have become friends and colleagues. We first met when I worked with Bronwen's mother, Judge Sondra Pardes, at a local politician's office in Queens, New York, in 1984. Bronwen was twelve at the time.

Fast forward to 2007: Bronwen is a young woman with a master's degree in human sexuality. She's also an experienced educator, and is the recent author of her first book, *Doing It Right*, a guide to sexuality for young adults. Coincidentally, I just happened to need the help of someone with Bronwen's skills. Simon Pulse was planning to publish a new edition of this book, and I hoped to find a sexuality expert to help me get the job done and to make certain that this non-expert did it right. I asked Bronwen if she could help, and I was very lucky that she said yes.

So thank you, Bronwen, for the opportunity to work with you, for bringing your keen eye, honest voice, and expertise to the preceding pages. I don't know where my words end and yours begin (and vice versa), and that's the kind of partnership every writer dreams of.

For more information about Bronwen and her work, please have a look at her website: www.doingitrightbook.com.

ACKNOWLEDGMENTS

I am beyond grateful to Miriam Altshuler for finding a new home for this second edition of *What If Someone I Know Is Gay?* And I'm equally grateful to the editors at Simon Pulse, including Bethany Buck, Michelle Nagler, and Sangeeta Mehta for providing that home.

Thank you as well to editorial assistants Caroline Abbey and Michael del Rosario for taking expert care of the many details that go into publishing a book.

For the original edition I am indebted to Jane O'Connor for commissioning this book in the first place; to Joel Fotinos for suggesting that I was the one to write it; and to my agent, Joy Harris, for encouraging me to do it.

Thank you especially to the many people who contributed their questions and thoughts and/or offered their help, support, and/or advice, including: Doug Aucoin; the late Dr. Betty Berezon; Sally Bourrie; Duffie Cohen;

acknowledgments

Dr. M. S. Frommer; Dr. Richard Hersh; Rachel Katz; Leslie Longenbough; Cynthia Lubow; Lewis, Maureen, and Ryan Marcus; Yona Zeldis McDonough; Stephen Milioti; Stuart Schear; Jonathan Schwartz; and Chris Tuttle.

Many thanks, as well, to those who read all or part of the manuscript and offered their valuable advice and comments. These include Dr. Leslie Bogen, Kate Chieco, Carolyn Cuttler, Cynthia Smith DiPalma, the late Arlene Eisenberg, Laura and John Foster, Kevin Jennings, Beth Karpfinger, Heidi Katz, Nancy Kokolj, Rochelle Lefkowitz, Chris Lord, Mynette and Richard Marcus, Brian McNaught, Penelope Tzougros, Pamela Wilson, and Evan Wolfson. I'm especially grateful to my friend Bob Weiss, who brought his keen eye and sound judgment to the pages of this new edition.

And, as always, for his love and unwavering support, thank you to my partner in life, Barney Karpfinger.

INDEX

index

Catch Alex Sanchez's novels, including the Rainbow series

"Groundbreaking."
—*Time Out New York*

"An important book for gay teens and their allies."
—*VOYA*

"The final installment of this trilogy is a true winner." —*SLJ*

"Inspired by the TV show *Queer Eye.*" —*PW*

Dr. M. S. Frommer; Dr. Richard Hersh; Rachel Katz; Leslie Longenbough; Cynthia Lubow; Lewis, Maureen, and Ryan Marcus; Yona Zeldis McDonough; Stephen Milioti; Stuart Schear; Jonathan Schwartz; and Chris Tuttle.

Many thanks, as well, to those who read all or part of the manuscript and offered their valuable advice and comments. These include Dr. Leslie Bogen, Kate Chieco, Carolyn Cuttler, Cynthia Smith DiPalma, the late Arlene Eisenberg, Laura and John Foster, Kevin Jennings, Beth Karpfinger, Heidi Katz, Nancy Kokolj, Rochelle Lefkowitz, Chris Lord, Mynette and Richard Marcus, Brian McNaught, Penelope Tzougros, Pamela Wilson, and Evan Wolfson. I'm especially grateful to my friend Bob Weiss, who brought his keen eye and sound judgment to the pages of this new edition.

And, as always, for his love and unwavering support, thank you to my partner in life, Barney Karpfinger.

INDEX